Finding Peace After a Suicide Loss

It's every parent's nightmare—the suicide death of a child. Elaine Kennelly has endured that nightmare. In her book *Finding Peace after a Suicide Loss: Healing Truths for Those Not Yet Healed*, she offers a path into daybreak, beyond bitterness to healing truths. We still understand little about depression and suicide even as society suffers these ills in increasing numbers. Elaine invites us into her insights, into her journey, into a better understanding of what seem impossible situations. Written in a then-and-now framework, *Finding Peace after a Suicide Loss* is balm for wounded spirits.

—Nancy E. Head,
author of *Restoring the Shattered: Illustrating
Christ's Love through the Church in One Accord*

I was stuck in grief after my nephew murdered both of his parents, my sister, and my brother-in-law. But this book, *Finding Peace after a Suicide Loss: Healing Truths for Those Not Yet Healed*, gave me hope that my nephew can be forgiven and reunited with his parents in heaven. My favorite point in the entire book is *grace always wins*!

—Teri Metcalf,
murder survivor and GriefShare participant

With honesty and transparency, Elaine Kennelly writes about the difficult-to-discuss topic of suicide in her book *Finding Peace after a Suicide Loss: Healing Truths for Those Not Yet Healed*. It's a topic she knows well. She doesn't sugarcoat the gut-wrenching pain survivors experience, and she doesn't say that the healing process is easy, but she shares significant truths that can help loved ones find peace after suicide loss. Her beautifully written words offer hope, comfort, and promise. Thank you, Elaine, for this important book!

—Twila Belk,
writer, speaker, and author of eight books, including,
The Power to Be, Be Still, Be Grateful, Be Strong, and *Be Courageous*

Finding Peace after a Suicide Loss: Healing Truths for Those Not Yet Healed is one of the more honest reflections concerning the loss of a loved one to suicide that I have ever read. The reader is immediately invited to walk with Elaine Kennelly through the depths of her brokenness and encounter a mother who has "darkness as her closest friend." This powerful journey leads one through this terrific battle of faith and redemption toward renewed faith in God expressed by prayer, service, and even a glimmer of hope. Elaine's vulnerability will empower you to open up your true heart to the Spirit as she teaches us to call upon God's hand to heal the soul.

—Rev. Dr. David R. Saliba,
Senior Pastor,
Perdido Bay United Methodist Church, Pensacola, Florida

In her book *Finding Peace after a Suicide Loss: Healing Truths for Those Not Yet Healed*, Elaine Kennelly unravels so many realities that were not understood after the suicide of my brother. I never understood the emotions I was going through until Elaine uncovered every single one of them through the pages of her helpful book. Thank you from the many people who will read this book and find comfort in knowing they aren't weak or crazy! They will know that God rescues them, and there is hope after all. I love you for opening up yourself and sharing your story to help others.

—Linda Jones,
suicide survivor in the loss of her brother

If there was ever a time for a book focusing gently but courageously on the subject of suicide, it is now. As a pastor for over sixty years, I would have bought this book for every situation involving a suicide. The increasing number of suicides among our youth and among senior adults is a staggering problem. This powerful book, *Finding Peace after a Suicide Loss: Healing Truths for Those Not Yet Healed*, can open up our hearts to make an eternal difference in the lives of people all around us. Is there any help or hope? Elaine Kennelly says yes! Our help and hope is Jesus! The timeliness and the transparency of this book on death by suicide are beyond amazing.

—Dr. Jimmy Jackson,
Pastor Emeritus,
Whitesburg Baptist Church, Huntsville, Alabama

In *Finding Peace after a Suicide Loss: Healing Truths for Those Not Yet Healed*, Elaine Kennelly has given an insightful, personal gift to counselors and clients who are trying to find or help facilitate peace after a suicide loss. This book provides the powerful use of Scripture as the ultimate healing truth and comfort for those wounded by grief and the spiritual devastation of suicide.

—Kathy Eggold,
Cofounder,
Cross Connections Counseling, Fort Wayne, Indiana

Finding Peace after a Suicide Loss: Healing Truths for Those Not Yet Healed is a definite biblical *must* for pastors and people struggling with surviving a suicide death.

—Pastor Al Braun,
St. Paul Minnesota Metro Circuit,
Lutheran Church, Missouri Synod

I highly recommend *Finding Peace after a Suicide Loss: Healing Truths for Those Not Yet Healed*. Christian pastors and lay leaders who are assisting people who have experienced the loss of a loved one by suicide will find this book to be very helpful. It is a resource that should be available to members of every congregation and Christian fellowship. Thank you, Elaine, for sharing your story and what the Lord has taught you in his Word as you have moved from profound loss to the peace that passes all understanding.

—Pastor Tom Eggold,
retired Lutheran minister

Raw and real—*Finding Peace after a Suicide Loss: Healing Truths for Those Not Yet Healed* is instrumental for gaining desperately needed insight and perspective with which to compassionately counsel patients and intimately relate to those who are struggling with the devastating, incomprehensible loss of a loved one through suicide.

—Dr. Tim O'Hara, MD, MPH

Finding Peace after a Suicide Loss: Healing Truths for Those Not Yet Healed is a heartfelt, transparent, healing story, engaging and easy to follow. Included in each chapter is a succinct "Healing Truth," which Elaine Kennelly unwraps for us. Her theology is solid. That she could find healing after such a tragedy gives hope to those who struggle after a suicide loss. She makes a good point about how suicide is not an unforgivable sin, which will bring comfort. I would encourage those who have experienced a suicide loss to read her story so they might also find healing. It is not an easy road, but Elaine has walked it successfully.

—Dr. Steve Hammer, MD

Beautiful! Powerful! Spiritual! Compelling! These words come to mind after reading *Finding Peace after a Suicide Loss: Healing Truths for Those Not Yet Healed.* I found that much of the content also applies to other grief causes, as I experienced with the loss of my wife. Praise God for his loving and helping hands in every wound not yet healed.

—Richard E. Maas,
retired Principal,
Grace Lutheran School, Menomonee Falls, Wisconsin

Finding Peace after a Suicide Loss: Healing Truths for Those Not Yet Healed is such a great answer for a time like this! Thank you, Elaine, for opening your life to us and being vulnerable, not only through the process of loss, but also into victory in Christ. You show us how God has taken you on a journey of healing, and you do it in a biblical way. What a great resource this will be among college ministries! I highly recommend it.

—Oliver Marin,
Student-Led Movements Team Leader with Cru, Latin America and the Caribbean

If you have been through the relentless grief of losing someone you love through suicide, *Finding Peace after a Suicide Loss: Healing Truths for Those Not Yet Healed* can be trusted as a guide through the guilt, despair, anger, and hopelessness that this loss brings into your life. Working through her own deep depression, emotional exhaustion, and faulty coping mechanisms, Elaine Kennelly finds the One she is most angry at is the One who is most present and patient with her to walk her slowly toward healing. Before her healing can be engaged, she has to learn to trust Jesus again. Without trite answers or faulty hope, Elaine offers her own faltering journey as evidence that there is a way through the darkness.

—Scott Slayback,
Pastor, LifeSpring Covenant Church, Loveland, Colorado

Elaine Kennelly's *Finding Peace after a Suicide Loss: Healing Truths for Those Not Yet Healed* is a raw and genuine journey from the pit of heartbreak in the aftermath of her son's suicide to the hope in a future as one who has overcome. The beauty of Elaine's story is the no-holds-barred journey through the pain to peace. Elaine shares her hurt, despair, and disappointment with God, exactly how anyone who has experienced this pain would expect. This is not a feigned Christian "how to get through this quickly to victory" kind of book. This is the story of the long sojourn in the company of a Father whose ways we don't always understand but always shows he is good.

—Rick Ebbers,
Pastor, The Journey Church—A Community Seeking God,
Longmont, Colorado

I cannot overstate the importance, compassion, and helpfulness of *Finding Peace after a Suicide Loss: Healing Truths for Those Not Yet Healed*. Elaine Kennelly understands the journey of healing because she has struggled with the severe loss of suicide. Despite the anguish and pain, she masterfully expresses the possibility of liberating peace on the other side of a suicide loss. Elaine's book is filled with powerful insights to assist you on your journey.

—Rev. Gary Brndiar, BCC,
Healthcare Chaplain

Finding
PEACE
After a
Suicide Loss

Healing Truths
for Those
Not Yet Healed

ELAINE
KENNELLY

NASHVILLE

NEW YORK · LONDON · MELBOURNE · VANCOUVER

Finding Peace After a Suicide Loss
Healing Truths for Those Not Yet Healed

© 2021 Elaine Kennelly

Published in New York, New York, by Morgan James Publishing. Morgan James is a trademark of Morgan James, LLC. www.MorganJamesPublishing.com

ISBN 9781631953514 paperback
ISBN 9781631953521 eBook
Library of Congress Control Number: 2020947707

Cover Design by:
Chris Treccani
www.3dogcreative.net

Interior Design by:
Christopher Kirk
www.GFSstudio.com

Morgan James is a proud partner of Habitat for Humanity Peninsula and Greater Williamsburg. Partners in building since 2006.

Get involved today! Visit
MorganJamesPublishing.com/giving-back

For words, dear God, I say thank you.
I dedicate these written words to those stag-
gering from the pain of a suicide loss:
  To those with doubt, anger, and fear;
  To those still struggling;
  To those not yet healed.
I offer these words as hope and healing with
trust in the Word incarnate, the Word made
flesh, the one who ultimately heals all wounds
and provides peace.

The LORD is close to the brokenhearted;
he rescues those whose spirits are crushed.
Psalm 34:18

Contents

Foreword

I met Elaine Kennelly when I spoke at a church in Loveland, Colorado. I could not articulate what I sensed when I first shook her hand, but as I have gotten to know her better, I have come up with this: Elaine emanates from her being the things that make life worth living—hope, faith, compassion, and joy. No wonder I feel energized each time I encounter her! But it is important to note that these life-giving things define who she is, not because of a carefree, problem-free existence; on the contrary, they have been the result of fire, of tragedy.

Our follow-up has been mostly through email. And sure, there has been the stuff of light conversation in our exchanges, but we have also gone to deep places as we have intentionally interacted with each other's writings. What we write about and our writing styles are vastly different from each other. I'm a missions scholar guy, and she's an inspirational writer. But as an author, I can usually detect authenticity (or the lack thereof) in other authors across genres. As I have gotten to know Elaine, I can unequivocally say that she is the real deal! By "authenticity" I mean that she is an author who allows real-life experiences to define and give shape to her writing. She is a writer courageous enough to share her doubts and struggles. She's a storyteller vulnerable with the reading public, enabling others to see who she is, imperfections and all.

In *Finding Peace after a Suicide Loss: Healing Truths for Those Not Yet Healed*, Elaine's authenticity comes shining through. In it she shares her and her husband's journey through an unimaginable tragedy—the suicide death of their son Matthew. To have sugarcoated the story with Christian niceties would have reeked of inauthenticity. Thank God she did not do that; instead, she invites us into the shock of profound loss and all the pain and anger and guilt and despair that accompany it in the long years afterward.

And it is from that place that Elaine Kennelly shares some wisdom with us. *Finding Peace after a Suicide Loss* is not a memoir, though after reading it, you will feel like you know the author. It is not a self-help book, though you'll likely feel more practically equipped to deal with crisis. To me, it is finally a guidebook based on the Sourcebook. Grounded in biblical wisdom and tested faith, this book is for those who find themselves dealing with tragedy of any kind but perhaps of the exact same kind. Suicide, unfortunately, is not as rare as we might think or hope.

I happened to read a prepublished version of the book just weeks after a missionary family received news of the suicide death of their seventeen-year-old son. Talk about a timely read. I bowed my head in deep gratitude to God for giving us the exact resource that our support team needed to minister to this hurting family. If we can count on anything in this life, it is that at some point each of us will experience loss, tragedy, despair of the deepest and life-altering kind. I believe Elaine's authentic insights will help many through such bleak seasons. *Finding Peace after a Suicide Loss* is a flashlight on a starless, moonless night.

Elaine, my friend, thank you for sharing with the world your difficult journey and all that you have learned (and continue to learn) from it. Thank you for showing us a way to endure trials, tribulation, and tragedy, and come out better for it. Thank you for sharing your soul so that others can find their way to Jesus—comforter of the mourning, healer of the broken, and giver of hope.

Dr. Al Tizon
Author, *Whole and Reconciled: Gospel, Church, and Mission in a Fractured World,* Executive minister, Serve Globally, Evangelical Covenant Church, Chicago, Illinois, Affiliate associate professor of Missional and Global Leadership, North Park Theological Seminary, Chicago, Illinois

Are *You* Not Yet Healed?

Nothing prepares us for a loved one's suicide.

All of us have been attacked by the same stunning sensation—the disbelief that such a horrible event could be happening.

All of us have a story to tell of shock and overwhelming pain and plaguing questions flooding our minds and tearing at our hearts.

Your loved one may have been your father or mother or a sister or a brother. Or he or she may have been your very own child—a son or a daughter. Maybe it was a spouse who completed suicide. Or perhaps your best friend.

You may have received the news, or even worse, you may have come upon the scene first.

My heart cries out for all of us who have experienced such a tragic and horrific loss.

Who can we go to?

Who will sustain us when the tears won't stop?

Who will share our pain?

Who will hear our story?

Who will understand?

How can *we* even understand what has happened and why?

How do we put the pieces of our lives back together?

Who will help us heal the hurts within us and among those in our family?

What can we do to restore the broken relationships and rebuild trust?

Can we ever find joy again in our lives?

I know how difficult it is to even think clearly enough to ask these questions and how difficult the answers we struggle with seem to be after a suicide. Our eighteen-year-old son Matthew snuffed out the life we cherished and loved. He was our precious son, and we loved him greatly! And yet, the relationship we thought was secure, Matthew changed. He replaced it with sorrow, guilt, rejection, blame, and doubt. His death broke my heart and spirit. It cloaked my life with repeated darkness, which in time became "my closest friend."[1]

Thirty years have passed since that awful day, and I survived what to me was unthinkable. Our marriage and the rest of our family survived too. The way through was often gut wrenching, but we did find our way to the other side. You can as well.

I am not a psychiatrist, psychologist, theologian, pastor, priest, or therapist. I am, however, a mom who survived the suicide death of her teenage son. I am the wife of a husband who lost his son. I am a mother of another son who lost his brother.

Through this journey of incredible loss, I can now recount to you what I have gained. Yes, I said gained. It's hard to imagine that anything so destructive and shocking can ever produce anything good. But it can—and not just in my life. As this book unfolds, I will share with you what I have received through such hurt. And I will show you what you can receive as well: a different and more peaceful life.

In the following pages, I will affirm your intense struggle as you attempt to put your life back together. I will also encourage you to know, without a doubt, you can live fully and happily once again. You can live in the freedom of forgiveness without the agony of suicide. You can live in the freedom of forgiveness without the continued mental anguish of suicide. You, too, can experience real joy. You, too, can come to understand and experience unlimited grace and the victory it has to offer you. I know you can enjoy these benefits in your life. Even through my loss of Matthew, I rediscovered the divine gift of absolute, unconditional grace. I came to know Jesus Christ in a much deeper, fuller way. Joy reentered my world once again.

My heart wants to shout "I made it!" And that would sound so proper.

I could sing "Victory in Jesus." Ahh, that would seem so easy.

I could tell how my prayers were answered—which would sound so ... well, Christian.

I can honestly say, though, that my victory over my son's suicide *does* belong to Jesus, and I *am* a Christian, but my process of healing has been arduous. Oh, what a word! Dictionaries define it as "difficult, requiring great physical or mental effort and skill, full of hardships, severe, taxing to the utmost." And that even sounds clinical in comparison to what I went through. Does it to you too?

Why is suicide suffering so intensely difficult to overcome? We survivors could gather up many different answers to this question. What I have come to see is that we are in a spiritual battle. Our faith and trust in God is battered, bruised, and broken. Our faith has been interrupted, like a power outage. The light in our lives has gone out. The surge of life we knew so well has abruptly stopped. We find ourselves in the dark, alone, without answers, afraid. We need life and light restored. But we know that they will not come to us in the form we had before. There's an empty chair at the table, a smile we'll never see in person again, a hand we can't hold, a voice we can't hear—except in our heads and hearts. We need emergency measures. We need something—someone—so we can keep going. So we can survive. So we can hopefully … finally … peacefully live again.

I want to share with you the truths God taught me through my loss. Through these truths, he restored light and life to my world. I want you to know his comfort, his encouragement, and his healing. I want you to see that you can follow him, that he hasn't abandoned you, that he hasn't been unfaithful to you. I want you to have joy again in your life!

Darkness may be your closest friend, even now. But you need not remain friends with darkness forever. There is a way back to the light, a way to have a life of peace. Let me show you what that is and how it can be yours.

PART ONE
THE DEATH

And I am convinced that nothing can ever separate us from
God's love. Neither death nor life, neither angels nor demons,
neither our fears for today nor our worries about tomorrow—
not even the powers of hell can separate us from God's love. No
power in the sky above or in the earth below—indeed, nothing
in all creation will ever be able to separate us from the love of
God that is revealed in Christ Jesus our Lord.

Romans 8:38–39

1

Sudden Sadness, Heavy Hearts

A Long Ago Yesterday

April 15, 1989

There I was in the "frozen tundra of the North," as I lovingly call it. The weather was unusual—a beautiful, sunshine-bright day and warmer. It was perfect for an April wedding in Wisconsin. In fact, I was driving home from one. I was upbeat and encouraged, happy. These country roads never have traffic, I thought to myself. So with the pedal to the metal, I turned up the volume on the radio and sang like no one was listening.

There was a lightness in my heart I hadn't known for a long time. Matthew seemed better to me, more stable, as though he had turned a corner. He seemed happier, calmer, and he smiled more.

Oh, I just know he's going to make it, I thought. What a story he will have. I even thought about what he would be able to say: God turned my life around. It was a mess, but God changed me. He did it all.

At that very moment, a beautiful rainbow appeared, sparkling, colorful, reaching heavenward! "Oh, Father God," I blurted out, and right there—in the middle of the road—I stopped, got out of the car, and lifted my hands in praise and thanksgiving. "Oh, Father, I am thanking you, in advance, for healing Matthew's severe depression. I know you gave this child to us as a special blessing, and I am taking this rainbow as a sign from you—like the promise you gave to Noah. I am putting my faith over my feelings, knowing you are going to heal him, and he will have a wonderful testimony of your faithfulness."

Two weeks later, Matthew was missing. He hadn't shown up at school or at work. He hadn't come home. None of his friends had seen him. My husband, Tom, searched frantically, but I wasn't worried. *God is taking care of this*, I reassured myself.

Two days later, Tom found Matthew. Dead. Our precious son had taken a heavy-duty extension cord from the garage and hung himself in the woods near our home. Tom brought me the tragic news at our church where, of all things, I was teaching a women's Bible class.

We had been thrust into the world of tragedy, and our lives would never be the same.

My life was shattered. Every thought was askew, like a train wreck sprawled out on the ground. Every bit of my heart was torn apart, mangled, crushed. I vividly remember the last hug

Matthew gave me—meaningful, heartfelt, not the least bit obligatory. It was a long, loving hug, one that I hadn't experienced in years.

What happened?

Where was Matthew's victory?

Where was his healing?

Where was God in all of this?

What brutally struck me was the total collapse of my beliefs. I felt as if I understood nothing. I felt completely abandoned, totally alone. Unloved. Rejected by Matthew. Spurned by God.

Devoid of certainty in all my beliefs, I screamed at God. "Hadn't I joyfully thanked you—for his healing—in advance?! Isn't that called trust? Isn't that called faith?"

Jesus had always been in my life. Just as it was for Ruth, Billy Graham's wife, I truthfully have no memories of ever living without Christ. My entire formal education was through Bible-believing, Christian schools, and I graduated from college as a Christian elementary school teacher. I had memorized many Bible verses, hymns, and catechism quotes, and I had taught numerous classes.

But everything I had ever learned about God was tested by Matthew's death. My life was changed forever.

"God, if this is what you are like, I want no part of you." I turned my back on him. "Just leave me alone" became my prayer.

I still went to church, but I didn't participate. *What difference did it make?* I concluded.

No one sat with our family in the pew. People avoided us. The pastor was no help either.

Christian comfort never showed up from friends or family.

Did I pray? Oh, I told God plenty, but none of it was positive. I felt isolated, deserted, and rejected, with no thought of recovery. Hope was gone.

Bible reading? Would that help? But then I thought, *What part of Scripture really explains suicide?* All I had were questions—but no answers and nowhere to find them.

Sorrow. Anger. Bitterness. Abandonment. Rejection. These are what I felt. These are what swallowed me whole.

How could God allow all of this to happen?

Today

Matthew died in the spring of 1989. Our culture's response to suicide hasn't changed much since then. Suicide is still rooted in the shame and guilt of the survivors. It is still a hushed conversation or, worse yet, no conversation at all.

Does the church respond any better? Not really. It is still busy categorizing sins, still avoiding the suicide issues that desperately need clarity.

What you need to know—and what I so desperately sought—is that there *are* answers. Our questions, our struggles, our frustration, hurt, and despair can be addressed. Our culture won't help, and too often our churches don't either. But in his Word, God *has* given us answers. And through his presence, he is ready to apply them—when we are ready to listen.

In each chapter, I will present one of these answers. I call them healing truths. They are simple truths, uncomplicated and straightforward. All of them are God's truths, and his truth never changes. Here is one of those truths:

A Healing Truth — In the battle with suicide, satan wins the first round.

Death over Life

As with all sin, it starts in the garden of Eden with the first couple, Adam and Eve, along with their children. They were the first family to show us how families operate. For the sake of clarity, let's assume their surname is First, the First Family. Although they were first, they didn't define or establish family. God did. The positions of husband, wife, father, and mother were hand-shaped by God, given his own breath. He gave them authority over his other earth-bound creatures. And with all of this going for them, the First Family still became overwhelmingly dysfunctional. Their first-born son was a murderer, snuffing out the tender life of his own brother, his own flesh and blood. The very first child conceived and born on Earth took a life in an act of violence and selfishness.[2]

What happened?

What went wrong?

Sin happened.

Human choice was used to go against God, and this changed everything.

Adam and Eve were above all of God's creation, just a little lower than the angels.[3] They lived freely in the magnificent garden of Eden, created specifically for them to enjoy. They talked with God daily and enjoyed walks with him in the cool of the day. The Bible does not tell us how long they lived in this idyllic environment. It could have been months, even years.

However long the time, Adam and his helpmate, Eve, governed it all, used it all, enjoyed it all, and ate all the fruit and vegetables they desired. Everything was available to them—except, that is, one tree in the middle of the garden.[4] Genesis 3 tells us how a serpent there—whom the Bible later identifies as the fallen angel satan—lied to Adam and Eve, deceived them, and led them to disobey God. [5] Satan won the first round in the human realm with God.

The fallout of that fateful human choice was awful. It alienated Adam and Eve from God, from the rest of the created order, and from each other.

Adam and Eve's disobedience delivered despair, disillusionment, and ultimately physical death. They lost their innocence. They were evicted from their home, made to grow their own food from ground now cursed, and felt shame for the first time in human history. But all was not lost. Before they were cast from Eden, they heard God tell them that satan would not win the war. One would come who would deliver a fatal blow to the evil one, and he would come through humanity, through the "seed" of the woman.[6] In other words, God would one day bring redemption and victory through a human family.

But so far in the biblical story, there's a human couple but no children, hence no full-blown family. God, however, sets this right outside of Eden. Strangely enough, even after their disobedience, God blesses Adam and Eve with children. He creates the First Family. And the first children are Cain and Abel.[7]

We know nothing about Cain and Abel's childhood, but in Genesis 4, we see that Cain grew up and became a farmer, while

Abel, his younger brother, was a shepherd. Both men bring an offering to God at harvest time.

> When it was time for the harvest, Cain presented some of his crops as a gift to the LORD. Abel also brought a gift—the best portions of the first-born lambs from his flock. The LORD accepted Abel and his gift, but he did not accept Cain and his gift. This made Cain very angry, and he looked dejected.[8]

God has a conversation with Cain, and he says, " 'What's wrong with you? Why do you have such an angry look on your face? If you had done the right thing, you would be smiling. But you did the wrong thing, and now sin is waiting to attack you like a lion. Sin wants to destroy you, but don't let it!' "[9]

In the very next verse, Cain invites his brother to go for a walk and promptly kills him!

God was right. Sin was waiting for Cain, and it did attack him like a lion.

Cain chose the path of death rather than life. He succumbed to blaming his brother rather than accepting responsibility for his own actions. He acted the way his parents had in Eden when, after sinning, they blamed others rather than themselves. We've been following this pattern ever since.

Sin came into the world through the disobedience of Cain's parents, and it has continued throughout every generation. We all live with sin, and it rots us from within. Sin attacks everyone, and the lead sinner, satan, encourages us to do the wrong thing, to make the wrong choice, to do what we know is wrong. Satan doesn't make us choose immorally, but, like a lion, he crouches in wait, lingering for opportunities to move us against God, which is also a move away from what is good for us.[10]

Sin is a part of suicide just as sin is a part of every wrong choice we make. As with Adam and Eve's disobedience, suicide holds a horrific consequence. There is no going back to the perfect Eden. Satan wins the first battle, I am sorry to say.

All Is Not Lost

Think about creation from God's perspective. All of his magnificent creation is on display. The universe, complete with star-studded galaxies, is bringing glory to God, its Creator. According to God's own evaluation, all of what he made began as "very good."[11] But as a consequence of sin, first in the angelic realm and then among humanity, God's good creation became marred. God's own children, Adam and Eve, made a devastating choice to exalt themselves.

Then God's grandchildren, Cain and Abel, could not get along. After Abel's death, even God asks a why question: " 'Why have you done this terrible thing? Your brother's blood is crying out to me from the ground, like a voice calling for revenge.' "[12] Even God hurts at that moment!

My dear suicide survivor, take comfort in the fact that God understands your despair, sadness, and questions. He put his magnificent creative power into the First Family, just as you have poured time, energy, discipline, love, hope, and dreams into your family. You invested in a marriage. You raised a child and lived with him or her. You may have even received a grandchild into your family, treasured that child, and developed a friendship with him or her. Whatever relationship you created and nurtured, you had it for years—until one day, one choice changed that forever. Just like Adam and Eve, your deceased loved one ate the fruit of free will gone wrong. Just like Cain, your loved one made the irreversible choice of taking a life.

From a human perspective, God has been there, right where you are now. God was there when sin entered the garden, and it seemed as though satan came out on top. God was there when Cain killed his brother, Abel, and it seemed as though satan won again. But God, in Jesus Christ, is the ultimate victorious One who, before creation, chose us to be holy and blameless.[13] And God promised us "before time began" that eternal life with him is always our hope.[14]

Satan may win the first battle, but God wins the war!

Father God, my loved one is gone, and I am trying to make sense of it all. I am crushed and full of sorrow. Please help me find comfort in you and your Word. Open my mind to read your counsel, to take it into my thought process, and to believe it. As one man who encountered Jesus said to him, " 'I do have faith, but not enough. Help me have more.' "[15] Also, help me understand family from your perspective, my Lord. Bless me with a deeper faith to understand your love for me and my loved one who chose death over life. Today, give me your comfort, your hope, and your peace. In Jesus's name I ask this. Amen.

2

Must I Choose
My Son's Casket?

A Long-Ago Yesterday

May 3, 1989

No one ever plans for this horrible day. No one even imagines what it must be like. It is thrust upon you with a vengeance. Today is the day we chose Matthew's casket.

Tom and I. No family. No friends. No music. No conversation. Just words from the funeral director droning on regarding fabric, wood, boxes, coverings, costs. Nothing made sense to me. What was I even doing here? Confusion reigned. I was alive, breathing, walking, and yet not comprehending.

What I remember is my inability to make a choice. My brain refused to work. You see, if I made a choice, I would have to admit that my son was dead. I couldn't take that risk. Maybe if I didn't choose, it never happened. Maybe this was all a mistake. I remember thinking, Let's go home. Matthew will be there, and this will all go away. But somehow, a choice was made, and it did not all go away.

Sudden death never goes away. There is no second chance, no do-over, no fresh start. One moment your loved one is alive, and the next they are gone forever from your earthly life, just like my dad who died of a sudden heart attack when I was only twenty-four years old. I remember the shock, the startling realization that he was gone … physically … forever.

Matthew's death held more heartache, more agonizing pain. To add the burden of a suicide death was more than I could handle. It was unthinkable, incomprehensible, unbelievable, inconsolable. That day, I wanted to die too.

Suicide pain shows no mercy. It haunts your thoughts excessively. The massive pain in suicide survival is that your loved one chose to leave. There, that is the crux of the problem—the choice. They make the choice to leave the family, the relationship, their own life—and all without your understanding why. We desperately want to know why!

Two years before Matthew's choice, I went through a season of depression. I wrote a note in my Bible, "1987—thoughts of suicide," next to this verse, "Unless the LORD had given me help, I would soon have dwelt in the silence of death."[16] While going through this deep depression, I had suicidal thoughts, and I distinctly remember thinking, *The easiest and best solution to this problem is suicide. If I were gone, things would be easier for everyone.*

The next memory I have was the *only* solution is suicide. For me, there was a logical progression from *a* solution to the *only* solution. I had a deep sense of hopelessness. Nothing was going to make this better because I could see no way out, no alternative route. My future was determined, set in stone. I would be helping the situation if I were not part of the present. Never once did I think about how my choice would affect anyone, let alone the husband whom I loved with all my heart and our children, whom I adored.

Hope was gone, and the only solution was lurking deep within, urging me to end my life. The Bible describes this perfectly: "Your will to live can sustain you when you are sick, but if you lose it, your last hope is gone."[17]

Today

Why did I not choose death? I don't know, but it probably was because I did not have major clinical depression recurring month after month, year after year. I wasn't mentally ill. I wasn't abusing drugs or alcohol. I believe God allowed me to participate in a season of depression to give me a better understanding of the suicidal thought process. Of course, I did not know that at the time. Two years later, after my son's death, I did.

The outcome of my depression is described in these verses from Psalm 94: "When I said, 'My foot is slipping,' your unfailing love, Lord, supported me. When anxiety was great within me, your consolation brought me joy."[18] I was eventually consoled, and my life continued.

A Healing Truth — God is always God, and he is sovereign.

Matthew is dead. I am alive.

I was healed. Matthew was not.

Why? I do not know.

The Bible explains, "The LORD our God has secrets known to no one. We are not accountable for them, but we and our children are accountable forever for all that he has revealed to us, so that we may obey all the terms of these instructions."[19] We don't know all the whys, but God does. He is all-knowing; we are not. He is eternally sovereign; we are not. All the answers are known, just not by us. And this can be incredibly frustrating.

But if we also believe that God is all-good and all-loving, then don't we also need to believe that he withholds certain information from us because it would not truly benefit us? Or that he keeps some answers to himself in order to help us in ways that are more important? He knows what we need more than we do. Can we trust in that?

The fact is, God *is* sovereign over all he has made, and we are among what he has created. Theologian Wayne Grudem says: "God's exercise of power over his creation is also called God's sovereignty. God's sovereignty is his exercise of rule, as 'sovereign' or 'king' over his creation."[20] In other words, God, as King, "does whatever he pleases,"[21] and what he pleases is always for our good.

The most famous biblical character called to suffer is Job, and Job clearly contends that "No one can oppose you [God], because you have the power to do what you want."[22] We could summarize Job's view this way: God is always God. His attributes include being all-powerful, all-knowing, present everywhere, faithful, and eternal. He is perfect. He is love, truth, and full of goodness. He is merciful, gracious, righteous, and worthy of our worship, praise, and thanksgiving. God is holy, just, and jealous. He is patient with us, and he offers us peace and rest. God is all these things and so much more.

When the Lord spoke to the prophet Jeremiah, he said, "I am the LORD God. I rule the world, and I can do anything!"[23] The New International Version says it this way: " 'I am the LORD, the God of all mankind. Is anything too hard for me?' " A rhetorical question at best because the answer is a screaming, "Of course not!" God is God, the great "I AM WHO I AM."[24] He cannot be less than he is, and he can never be overtaken or outwitted.

God is in charge, but everything that happens is not what he desires. He is in control, but he is not all-controlling. He doesn't make our choices for us, but he does respond to them. And his responses are always the best and wisest, even when we don't understand what he is up to. While I know God is in charge, I also know that I will never be able to figure him out. And that, my dear friends, is the struggle. But here is what I do understand:

> Have you ever come on anything quite like this extravagant generosity of God, this deep, deep wisdom? It's way over our heads. We'll never figure it out. Is there anyone around who can explain God? Anyone smart enough to tell him what to do? Anyone who has done him such a huge favor that God has to ask his advice? Everything comes from

him; Everything happens through him; Everything ends up in him. Always glory! Always praise! Yes. Yes. Yes.[25]

The More We Need

Back in 2012, I wrote these words in a prayer journal, as though God were speaking to me:

"Elaine, my words are total truth, and this is important. My words are true, written by people, but with my Holy Spirit to guide them. When you read the Bible, you can rest assured, and have total confidence, that I am talking to you. Of course, it is a condensed version because you cannot fully comprehend me. I am even bigger and better and beyond the Bible. I am more than you can understand."

GOD Is Always MORE

God and His vastness is more than I can see,
More than you or I could ever hope to be.
Why, if I could, for just a day or two
Comprehend His being....NO
That—I could never do.

The magnitude of God is more than I can feel
More than you or I could ever hope to reveal.
Why, If I could, for just a day or two
Know His magnitude....NO
That—I could never do.

Unfathomable is He; more than I can take in, is He.
More than you or I could ever hope to be.
Why, if I could, for just a day or two
Understand His mind....NO
That—I could never do.

You see, if I could perhaps understand or comprehend
The mind of God, His being, without beginning or end,
Then.....I would BE God,
And that—I could never do.

How tragic to make God so small
That we should understand His ways.
How sad to have a God that is
Puny, insufficient and ceases to amaze.

How naive to pretend that God is only
As big as my mind can understand.
How happy I am that my God has the
Whole of creation at His command!

YES, my God is bigger and grander
And deeper and higher than all,
And my mind is puny and shallow
And petty and small.

> Praise God for His magnitude,
> We can NOT comprehend!
> Praise God whom we worship,
> Adore, and trust...without end.

Declaring God as sovereign ruler gives him the name Lord or Master. He is the potter; I am the clay. He is the vine; I am the branch. He leads; I follow. It means trusting him in every circumstance of life. Even through a suicide? Yes, especially through a suicide, because there are no clear answers to questions we feel compelled to ask.

You see, the sovereign God we call Father understands our questions. He is longing for us to come to his throne and ask boldly, "How could you allow this to happen? You could have stopped it, prevented it, diverted it, changed it ... but my loved one is dead. Where were you, Lord?"

The answer to that question takes us to the sovereignty of God, and our surrender to the answer is the answer. Here is how God describes himself:

> "My thoughts are nothing like your thoughts,"
> says the LORD. "And my ways are far beyond anything
> you could imagine. For just as the heavens are higher
> than the earth, so my ways are higher than your ways
> and my thoughts higher than your thoughts."[26]

Dear Father, as you well know, I have asked the why questions over and over. Forgive my hard heart. I am selfish and desire an easier path than you have chosen for me. I desire the secret answers that only YOU know and understand. Maybe some day you will share them with me, but for today, I humbly bow before you, surrendering my questions, my doubts, and all my sorrow. You are MORE than I am able to understand. How wonderful is that! Thank you for being the ultimate, magnificent, sovereign King of kings and Lord of lords, fully in control of all. Infuse me with your life-giving Spirit that I may become all that you desire for me. In the powerful name of Jesus, I ask. Amen.

3

The Wake and the Worship

A Long-Ago Yesterday

May 4, 1989

This is the day we celebrated Matthew's life. It was his funeral. The choice of an open casket was easy. I was desperate to see him one last time.

I thank God we chose casual, outdoor clothes for Matthew to wear. He was the fisherman in our family. I still remember the bold red and black squares on his flannel shirt with his favorite blue T-shirt underneath. We didn't dress him with a stiff collar, tie, or sport coat. Instead, we chose his favorite jeans, his favorite shirts, all very much against protocol for a proper funeral three decades ago, but I'm so happy we did.

An employee of ours, using beautiful calligraphy, created a plaque that we put into the open casket. It read:

For I am convinced that nothing can ever sepa-
rate us from his love. Death can't, and life can't. The
angels won't, and all the powers of hell itself cannot
keep God's love away. Our fears for today, our worries
about tomorrow, or where we are—high above the sky,
or in the deepest ocean—nothing will ever be able to
separate us from the love of God demonstrated by our
Lord Jesus Christ when he died for us.[27]

It was nestled into the corner, right above Matthew's long, curly
hair. Everyone had to see it. It was the only thing that made truthful
sense that night.

The wake was scheduled prior to the church service. Hundreds
gathered. So many teenagers. Our little church expanded out into
the street. The line inside was long. We were overwhelmed. I felt
we were the ones reassuring everyone who came. Somehow, against
all odds, the Holy Spirit breathed into Tom and me the power to
comfort others.

The service was upbeat, and much to my surprise, I did not cry.
Two of our dearest friends came hundreds of miles to sing a beautiful
duet. The hymns sung were joyful. The sermon was powerful, based
on the frustration of Paul in Romans 7:19–20: "I want to do what
is good, but I don't. I don't want to do what is wrong, but I do it
anyway. But if I do what I don't want to do, I am not really the one
doing wrong; it is sin living in me that does it."

There was hope for all Christians that evening, in and through
Jesus Christ, and that was our intent, for the gospel to be preached,
for God to be worshiped, for Matthew's life to be celebrated because
we knew where he was, with his Savior, Jesus, in heaven. We knew,

without doubt, because Matthew believed in God and the saving grace of Jesus. Scripture says, "Believe in the Lord Jesus and you will be saved."[28] "But to all who believed him and accepted him, he gave the right to become children of God."[29]

At the end of the service, Tom and I addressed those who came, and we shared personal thoughts. I spoke specifically to the young people, Matthew's friends and acquaintances who had come. Matthew had made many poor, in fact, dangerous choices as a teenager. He had used marijuana and other illegal drugs. I spoke, addressing that issue. Tom spoke regarding salvation through faith in Christ. The Holy Spirit gave us both what was needed at the moment to do something both of us deeply desired to do.

A Healing Truth — Worship God, even in the midst of severe sorrow.

After a suicide, you desperately need to worship.

Despite our sadness, we were able to worship at our son's funeral. It seems like a contradiction, but the singing, the praying, and listening to the message all lifted us up in the midst of a crushing blow, a serious injury to our marriage and to our family. Everyone present was faced with questions and uncertainty. Even the pastor didn't have all the answers. But the one thing we did have was the presence of God. He was in that place.

We offered up what we had to give, meager at best. It was our heart and the motive of our hearts. It was our sincere desire to share Jesus in the midst of a severe tragedy. Worship does that. It is an offering, an expression of our love and commitment to God. It brings him glory, and he delights in it. The Bible says, "let us go right into the presence of God with sincere hearts fully trusting him."[30] Even in our suffering, we went right into the presence of God that night, and a loving Father reached out to us with strength for us to complete the task.

Today

Worship offers a promise to everyone: "Come close to God, and God will come close to you."[31] God will minister to you in the depths of your sadness, and God's Holy Spirit will comfort you and provide strength for you to grieve and ultimately heal. That is a promise that hasn't changed through the ages. Worship will allow you to receive the gifts of strength and healing because it pleases God when you worship him. " 'The LORD your God is living among you. He is a mighty savior. He will take delight in you with gladness. With his love, he will calm all your fears. He will rejoice over you with joyful songs.' "[32]

How do you continue to worship after the funeral? Be forewarned: it is difficult but not impossible. Remember, " 'nothing is impossible with God,' "[33] and we are his in Christ.

———————

Heavenly Father, suicide poses many questions, with very few answers, and it is a difficult death for survivors like me to overcome. I thank you for opportunities to worship you daily, in the Word, in song, in prayer, with others, or all by myself. Without a doubt, you are always with me. I take great comfort in your presence. I may not always feel loved, but I know you love me, you forgive me, and you are preparing a place for me in heaven, just as you did for my loved one. I am a forgiven child of God, and I come to you now, resting in your love and forgiveness in Jesus's name. Amen.

4

Cold Ground, Bitter Hearts

A Long-Ago Yesterday

May 5, 1989

Strange as this may sound, I was upbeat after the funeral. I was refreshed, encouraged. Matthew was in heaven, and we had celebrated. I slept that night for the first time in days.

But Matthew's burial service was today, and there was no celebration.

It was a lousy weather day, cold and gray and windy. The ceremony was brief, and I do not remember one word, one thought, one God-inspired moment. It was as though God skipped this part of the process. Where was the comfort I was supposed to receive from him? Where was the comfort from my family and my friends? I can remember no words, no sympathy, no kindnesses, spoken or otherwise. It was a horrible day—nothing but sadness, overwhelming sadness.

The reality of what had happened set in, and the heaviness of living with this sadness weighted my thoughts and crushed my heart. I thought of Matthew being in the cold ground. I hated that thought. The wind was cold. I was cold, tugging at the coat that never brought warmth. Even my soul was cold. I looked at the closed casket, and all I could see was rejection—my own son rejected me. I felt cheated and betrayed by God, my family, my friends, my church, even Matthew's doctors. There was no one who bypassed my scathing anger, my mistrust. I didn't even recognize God in my thoughts. Where was the God I knew? He certainly wasn't there, and I didn't even care.

Guests came to our house. A huge mistake, but that's what was done years ago in my family culture; it was what was expected of us. Our fourteen-year-old son, now our only child, wanted his friends at the house. How could I refuse? There was conversation, chatter, lunch was being served, plates clattering, even laughter. It was incredulous to me! My life had caved in, never to be the same, and everyone around me was acting as though nothing had happened! How could they even think of eating? Food seemed repulsive to me. People were repulsive to me. Life was repulsive to me!

Filled with sudden rage, I desperately wanted to scream, "Get out of my house ... out of my life ... let me be alone ... let me be dead, too!" I wanted to weep and weep and weep until I died. But I said nothing and I did nothing, putting on the invisible mask of compliance. The anger was politely pushed deep inside. The only words of comfort I ever remember from my mother were "Be strong, Elaine. Be strong." There were women there who I thought were friends, actually talking about their children's high school graduation scheduled at the end of the month, and my future graduate had just been buried in the cold, dark, ugly ground.

If Matthew's funeral service was held in the presence of God, his burial day was the absence of God. I think that's called hell.

A Healing Truth — God's presence is not dependent on our circumstances or feelings.

Today

My friends, suicide will bring out the worst in you. There is this huge hole, this gap in your understanding between what you believe and what actually happened. What I fervently believed was God loved me and that Matthew would be healed. What actually happened was my son took his own life, and God allowed it. This gulf of disparity is at the foundation of every suicide survivor's struggle.

God led me to Oswald Chambers, an author who has taught me so much. He wrote the words in the widely read devotional *My Utmost for His Highest*. Here is one of my favorite excerpts: "Satan does not tempt us just to make us do wrong things. He tempts us to lose what God has put into us through regeneration, namely the possibility of being of value to God. Satan does not come to us on the premise of tempting us to sin, but on the premise of shifting our point of view."[34]

Satan did that in the garden of Eden, and he did it again with Jesus. The ancient physician and Gospel writer Luke takes us on a journey into the wilderness with Jesus. First of all, satan tries to tempt Jesus by saying to him, " 'If you are the Son of God, tell this stone to become a loaf of bread.' "[35] Did you hear the shift in satan's point of view? Of course Jesus *is* the Son of God and satan knows that. What did he mean by saying "if"? Then two more times satan lies and attempts to change the words of God to fit his own evil schemes. On each occasion, Jesus replies back to satan using Scripture, the crucial element in this encounter.[36]

God's words are truth. He cannot lie.[37] So when satan tempts you to change your point of view—and he will—what ammunition do you have in *your* arsenal? What words from God do you have in *your* mind? You won't always have a book or device at your fingertips to search for Bible passages that can help you. And satan will tempt you often, especially as you are emotionally and spiritually weak after your loved one dies. The good news is that your mind can hold your ammo!

Medically, I am no expert, only a mom. All I have is my experience. But I would venture to say that after a suicide death, the survivor's brain stops functioning logically and methodically. Following a suicide, survivors feel confusion, and they experience difficulty thinking clearly. Their memory seems temporarily damaged. In my case, I did remember a few words from Scripture: "I will never leave you nor forsake you."[38] These eight words were enough for a while. Then six more came to mind: "God is our refuge and strength."[39] I could recall only fourteen words, but they were my ammunition, my help, when I needed to quickly refute the lies of satan.

Take comfort in this fact: God is present in the words he gives to us. Discover Bible verses that speak to your heart and repeat them often throughout the day. You will be glad you did.

God with Us

God was at the burial site even though I did not feel he was. God is always present. One of his attributes is omnipresence, meaning everywhere present.[40]

We are never alone, forsaken, abandoned, or left on our own, even when we feel otherwise. Feelings are always in a state of flux; they are temporary, changing hour by hour. They can be right. They can be wrong. Most of the time, they are neither. They just are. That's the trouble with feelings; they are nebulous. But God's Word is not. We can trust it to be truth. Jesus said, "I am the way, the truth, and the life."[41] We can always trust him, and as God, he is omnipresent. Everywhere we are, he is. So we can rest fully in his presence no matter how we feel.

Precious Jesus, thank you for demonstrating to me how to respond to satan's treachery and lies. Thank you for giving me your example to follow. Give me the determination to follow through on knowing and memorizing your words so I will have power over satan's lies. Thank you for your daily presence with me. I am never alone. I am never abandoned. Even though I am struggling, I know you are my strength. In Jesus's name, I thank you. Amen.

5

Life Continues by Choice

A Long-Ago Yesterday

May 6, 1989

Yesterday, we buried our older son. Today, our youngest goes to the Junior Prom.

It was like that with Matthew and Nathan all along. They were at opposite ends of our family's dynamics. One was introverted; one was the extrovert. One looked at life as the glass totally empty; the other saw the glass as full and fun. Matthew was melancholy. Nathan was sunshine. They were both adopted as babies, but they were not siblings. One felt rejected by his birth mother. The other was happy to have two moms.

"So how does a freshman get to go to the Junior Prom?" That was the question posed to me in the fall of 1988. You see, Nathan was already working on that option. As I explained to him, "Only

Juniors go to the Junior prom; however, if a junior should ask you, a freshman, to go to the prom, you, too, could go." Music to his ears.

That is what awaited us on Saturday, May 6th. There was a tux to be picked up and shoes, and don't forget the corsage. What about transportation? Oh, yes, her father is driving. Oh, yes, they know we just buried Matthew. It puts a damper on the word "festivity," doesn't it?

But life goes on.

You think after a sudden death that your life can never go on, but in reality, your heart is still beating, and your lungs are still breathing in air. It's your mind that refuses to go to the next day. In my mind, I did not want to move on. I did not want to think about a prom.

What I wanted to do was wallow in death and darkness and never get out of bed again. My desire was to stop my life as I knew it and remain submerged in my own misery. I really didn't want to mother and nurture and get excited about my freshman son going to the Junior Prom! I felt I deserved misery, because somewhere along the line, I had failed miserably.

A Healing Truth — In the battle with suicide survival, choose life—daily.

Moses, at eighty years of age, was called into the ministry. Against all odds, he led the Hebrew people out of Egypt, and you can read his story in the book of Exodus.

Forty years after God called him to be a leader and shortly before his death, Moses spoke to the Hebrew people prior to their entry into the Promised Land. Here is part of what he said:

"Today I have given you the choice between life and death, between blessings and curses. Now I call on heaven and earth to witness the choice you make. Oh, that you would choose life, so that you and your descendants might live! You can make this choice by loving the LORD your God, obeying him, and committing yourself firmly to him. This is the key to your life."[42]

He wanted the people to choose life. He pleaded with them to make that positive choice. This is the choice God always wants his people to make, including you. Choose life! Yes, you, the survivor. The temptation while you are suffering and grieving is to ignore life. You will not want to participate. You will not want to even smile, let alone laugh. You will not want to celebrate a birthday, let alone go to a party. You will not want to get dressed, let alone go to work. You are exhausted, deeply hurt, confused, angry, and so much more. Life seems bleak and harsh. And you tend to give in to that, preferring darkness over light, dread over life. But you don't need to stay in the dark with death. You can venture into the light and choose life again.

Thank goodness I didn't have to attend the prom. I only had to choose life before the prom in the comfort of our living room. Nathan looked so grown up, so handsome in a tux. We took lots of pictures, and then his beautiful date arrived with her dad. I distinctly remember, they both were kind in their words to us. Everyone managed to smile, and there were more pictures. Prom night proved to be fun for Nathan and his date. It all turned out well because we chose life.

Today

We chose what we had over what we had lost. We chose what was best for Nathan and his life that night, even though we had just buried his brother. Choosing life is choosing to love, even when you do not feel loving. It is making unselfish choices without demanding anything in return. Choosing life reminds me of these words in 1 Corinthians 13:6, "[Love] does not rejoice about injustice but rejoices whenever the truth wins out." Injustice was the loss of Matthew, but the truth that won out was the blessing of Nathan—going to the prom.

Oswald Chambers writes, "Our yesterdays hold broken and irreversible things for us." The death of your loved one is irreversible, but there is a way to choose life. "God can transform this destructive anxiety into a constructive thoughtfulness for the future. Leave the broken irreversible past in God's hand, and step out into the invincible future with him."[43] If you are in the first stages of suicide grief, "a constructive thoughtfulness for the future" is not easy. In fact, I would say it is impossible without a miraculous gift from God. As I look back on my first week of suicide grief, the death, the discovery, the funeral, and the burial, I know now that a huge battle looms before you. But I also know that God will transform your "destructive anxiety," your personal battle, "into a constructive thoughtfulness for the future." You *will* have joy again in your life.

Dear God, the Father of Abraham, Isaac, and Jacob, you are my God too. I find myself in a daily battle as I make choices. I desire life and joy and healing, but many days I am wallowing in my misery. Forgive me, Father, for choosing darkness over light. "Create a clean heart in me, O God, and renew a faithful spirit within me. Do not force me away from your presence, and do not take your Holy Spirit from me. Restore the joy of your salvation to me, and provide me with a spirit of willing obedience."[44] *I desire to heal, Father. Help me through this difficult time. In Jesus's name. Amen.*

PART TWO
THE BATTLE

God is strong, and he wants you strong. So take everything
the Master has set out for you, well-made weapons of the best
materials. And put them to use so you will be able to stand up
to everything the Devil throws your way. This is no afternoon
athletic contest that we'll walk away from and forget about in
a couple of hours. This is for keeps, a life-or-death fight to the
finish against the Devil and all his angels.

Ephesians 6:10–12 MSG

6

Overwhelming Sorrow

A Long-Ago Yesterday

1989–1990

We stayed in our home for the first year following Matthew's death. Matthew had lived there for fourteen years, and he loved the lake bordering our property. We still call it the Lake House. I thought I would live there forever; after all, this is where Matthew grew up. Vivid memories flooded every room. Family pictures raced up the stairway. His bedroom was still filled with … well, him. Why would I ever move away?

I often went into his closet and openly wept into his clothing. I could still smell his aftershave. I could feel his presence, and I imagined him there with me. I found that comforting. I often sobbed uncontrollably, but it was an avenue of grieving for me, especially when I was alone in the house. It was just Matthew and me, and I could imagine he was still alive.

Food became an issue with me. At first, nothing tasted good, and I had no appetite whatsoever. I just couldn't eat. Sorrow and grieving can cause you to forget to eat, but for me, it went beyond that. Food was the one thing I could absolutely control. You see, my life was now completely out of control. Everything was different—suddenly and forever. And by not eating, I had control over something. I became obsessed with weight loss and being thin. Eating was an issue for me for years. I skipped meals. Made excuses. Started running. Lost weight, until I was only ninety pounds. And when the scale shouted back "eighty-nine," I finally understood my death wish.

For some in my family, life seemed to go on. Nathan was happy going back to school, with social events and friends around him. That first summer, he became a golf caddy and loved it.

Tom really had no choice. He had to return to work, and he was able to function well. He and Nathan would go golfing, or he would take Nathan and his friends out in the boat, tubing and water-skiing.

While Nathan and Tom lived forward, I floundered. I didn't go back to work. I didn't care about work. I didn't care about anything. I didn't desire to help another soul, and I chose isolation rather than interaction. I chose to be alone, and depression quickly engulfed me.

In those early months of sorrow, I had no one at my side. During the day, I would stay in bed, trying to sleep and forget; trying to pray, but I couldn't; trying to comprehend, but confusion reigned. I could not think clearly. I had no one to cry with, no one to listen, no one to pray with, no one to talk with. *If only someone would be here with me*, I thought. *Father God, where are you?* But even he didn't answer. I felt total abandonment and extreme weariness, as though my spirit had died along with Matthew.

Where was the Elaine I knew? She was gone. In her place was the hollow being of one in despair.

Nothing was the same.

Nothing seemed to matter.

Nothing was good and kind.

Even my beautiful relationship with Tom was cold and dead. He could not comfort me, nor could I comfort him.

The real struggle of losing a child is neither spouse has anything left to give. Both are hurting to such a degree that the relationship melts down to the sheer survival of self.

At the time, we were told that 94 percent of all married couples whose child completed suicide ended in divorce. That cold, hard statistic was understandable. Tom and I had had a strong and fun marriage. When one was down, the other was up. Life was good. We were happy. We loved each other. We adored each other. Yes, we had trials, but we made our way through them. And yes, other problems surfaced too, but they were always fixable. So where was the marriage I thought I knew? That, too, was gone. Tom and I now hardly talked, and when we did, blame often crept in to the conversation. Finger-pointing reared its ugly head. *You should have ... You could have ... Why didn't you?* In a suicide death, blame will always accompany the survivor. It is inevitable. Destructive. Demeaning. It plays havoc with a healthy relationship.

Still, our prayer as a couple became *Oh, Lord, keep us in the 6 percent.*

A Healing Truth—There is One who understands your sorrow.

I found it difficult to read Scripture those first years after Matthew died. I didn't trust it. I was plagued by anger, confusion, and doubt, but one Bible book still connected with me—Psalms. Its poetry is filled with emotion, with the ups and downs of life. Anyone who has grieved over a death, any death, understands the range of human emotions. One moment you can feel fine, and the next you are plunging into the depths of sadness. I plunged into Psalm 88 and stayed there. Here are some verses I clung to:

> I am overwhelmed with troubles
>   and my life draws near to death.
> I am counted among those who go down to the pit;
>   I am like one without strength. …
> Your wrath lies heavily on me;
>   you have overwhelmed me with all your waves.
> You have taken from me my closest friends
>   and made me repulsive to them.
> I am confined and cannot escape;
>   my eyes are dim with grief.
> But I cry to you for help, Lord;
>   in the morning my prayer comes before you.
> Why, Lord, do you reject me
>   and hide your face from me? …

> You have taken from me [my son] ...
>   darkness is my closest friend. [45]

These are sorrowful words. This entire psalm expresses grief, pain, loneliness, and depression. Prior to Matthew's death, I had never read it. I had never heard a sermon or a speaker mention Psalm 88.

Nine years into our grief, in the country of Israel, standing in the place where Jesus was beaten and mocked, our tour guide, Tony, said, "This is the place believed to be where Jesus was imprisoned on Thursday night, and in the darkness of his prison, I believe that Jesus recited Psalm 88." I remember physically gasping! Jesus ... sorrow ... Psalm 88. That was the moment I knew Jesus understood me and my intense suffering. Standing in that spot, I understood a little more about him and what he had endured.

Many Christians tend to teach that the sorrow of Jesus began in the garden of Gethsemane. I would beg to differ. I believe Jesus's suffering started when he had to leave heaven. Imagine the sorrow Jesus felt when he, the almighty God of the universe, voluntarily left his place of supreme glory to become a human infant, a helpless baby, born into a poor, uneducated family, in a dirty stable meant for animals. This is how author Sarah Young describes it, placing the words on the lips of Jesus:

> "Try to imagine what I gave up when I came to
> earth as a baby. I set aside My Glory, so that I could
> identify with mankind. I accepted the limitations
> of infancy under the most appalling conditions—a

filthy stable. That was a dark night for Me, even
though angels lit up the sky, proclaiming 'Glory' to
awe-struck shepherds."[46]

Over seven hundred years before Jesus was born, the
prophet Isaiah described Jesus this way: "There was nothing
beautiful or majestic about his appearance, nothing to attract
us to him. He was despised and rejected—a man of sorrows,
acquainted with deepest grief. … Yet it was our weaknesses he
carried; it was our sorrows that weighed him down."[47] Jesus's
own words show us the depth of his feelings: "The sorrow in
my heart is so great that it almost crushes me."[48] On Thursday
night, just before Jesus was arrested in Gethsemane, he asked
his disciples to pray with him. They didn't. Instead they all fell
asleep. When the temple guards came to arrest Jesus, his disciples all ran away. He was deserted by his dearest and closest friends. Later that night, one disciple even betrayed him.
Another denied him. All left him.

During his crucifixion, John, the only disciple among the
closest twelve, his mother, sister, and another female follower,
stood near to him during his dying moments. And in the final
seconds of his life, Jesus called out, " 'My God, my God, why
have you forsaken me?' "[49] He recited Psalm 22:1. He remembered the words of the Psalm writer and used them as he cried
out in agony to his Father.

Take heart, my friend. Jesus understands your sense of rejection, your grief, your sorrow, and your estrangement from God.
That is the truth, regardless of your feelings.

Today

There are numerous verses from the Psalms that will touch your heart with cries of sorrow and sadness. Search the Psalms for words that will cry out as prayers for you personally. Here are several I read over and over and over:

> — "I cried out to God for help; I cried out to God to hear me. When I was in distress, I sought the LORD; at night I stretched out untiring hands, and I would not be comforted."[50]

> — "O LORD, how long will you forget me? Forever? How long will you look the other way? How long must I struggle with anguish in my soul, with sorrow in my heart every day? How long will my enemy have the upper hand?"[51]

> — "I say to God my Rock, 'Why have you forgotten me? Why must I go about mourning, oppressed by the enemy?' "[52]

> — "O LORD, don't rebuke me in your anger or discipline me in your rage. Have compassion on me, LORD, for I am weak. Heal me, LORD, for my bones are in agony. I am sick at heart. How long, O LORD, until you restore me?"[53]

— "He heals the brokenhearted and bandages their wounds."[54]

— "The LORD cares deeply when his loved ones die."[55]

— "I am worn out waiting for your rescue, but I have put my hope in your word."[56]

— "The LORD helps the fallen and lifts those bent beneath their loads."[57]

— "I will bless the LORD who guides me; even at night my heart instructs me. I know the LORD is always with me. I will not be shaken, for he is right beside me."[58]

— "The LORD is close to all who call on him, yes, to all who call on him in truth."[59]

Embrace the Psalms. Every emotion you can imagine is expressed in this inspired book of poetry and song. And even through expressions of heartbreaking sorrow and deep despair, you will also find God's love and comfort. Wherever you are on the road to healing, you can find yourself in the Psalms.

Jesus, sweet Jesus, you know my sorrow and understand my sadness.
I do find comfort in that. You care for me. Thank you for giving up
your glory and becoming a human being. For the days when I am
especially weak in spirit, help me to overcome. Help me read your
Word, even when I don't feel like it. Help me recognize your pres-
ence, even when I don't feel it. I want to win the war in this battle
with suicide survival. I want joy again in my life, and I know your
Holy Spirit can change me, if I desire it. Fill me with your goodness
and love, which I so desperately need. Thank you. Thank you. Thank
you ... in the precious name of Jesus. Amen.

The Arms of Jesus

Oh, that I could cry in church ...
Allow my heart to weep and sob.
My life is crushed and broken.
Are you here with me, dear God?

Where are Your arms around me?
I stand stiffly all alone.
Tears well up within my eyes,
And inwardly I groan.

Can't hold the hurting arrows
Of the grief inside my soul.
Piercing pain is too much now
I sob without control.

Weeping ... hoping ... *someone*
Would turn and weep with me.
Would put their hand inside of mine.
Would be the Jesus I could see.

Will you be one who comforts?
Will you wipe away a tear?
And pray over a crippled soul?
Or are you frozen, filled with fear?

Fear of awkward moments—
Not knowing what to do.
Just be the arms of Jesus,
Let *His* love flow through you.

7

Oh God, Just Leave Me Alone!

A Long-Ago Yesterday

1990–1997

These years were insanity. I was not in my right mind. The first year of grief is typically about sorrow and sadness, finding your "new normal." But suicide grief is different. It's filled with confusion, and I found that I was not able to get back into a rhythm of life that held peace for me. I had sudden bursts of temper. Or I was wallowing in self-pity, unable to think clearly, ambushed by memories, haunted by Matthew's physical death, plagued by guilt. I was struggling in so many facets of my life: marriage, parenting, work. I was also still struggling with God. My cherished beliefs were challenged, and I doubted the very core of my faith.

With how difficult and strenuous all this was, I got to the place where I didn't have it in me anymore to fight and question God. And, unfortunately, I just gave up trying to resolve my issues with him and find reconciliation.

When I went to the cemetery, I found no comfort there either. I only felt duty-bound to go. I felt compelled to put flowers there. I thought I would find peace. But I didn't. The sad truth was that I fell apart, completely, every time I visited the gravesite. For me, it was never a time of peace, just intense sadness and a flood of tears. It broke my heart every time. So I stopped going.

I had honest questions with no answers. I was struggling spiritually with my envy, my guilt, and my anger. I was hopeful one day and hopeless the next. I missed Matthew in my daily life, having him around the dinner table, celebrating holidays and birthdays with him. I agonized over the thought of never getting to go to his wedding or hold his children. I was on an emotional roller coaster, and as each day began, I was not sure if I would be on the crest of the high point or in the valley of despair. It was an awful way to live.

Our local church failed us miserably. They were of no help whatsoever. That was hurtful, but understandable. After all, they were just people.

What rocked my world to the core, however, was that I believed God had failed me too. Remember, I had prayed out loud, standing under God's rainbow, putting my faith on the line and trusting in his goodness. I had thanked God in advance for the gift of healing Matthew, the child he had chosen for us. And now my child was dead—and by suicide! How could I comprehend this new reality with God? How could I live with this dichotomy?

I screamed at God in anger.

I begged him to tell me why.

I pleaded for his answers.

I searched his Word.

I stormed the gates of heaven.

And what I got in return was silence. Empty, screaming, shattering silence.

I closed my heart and mind to God.

I turned away from Jesus, my best friend, and said to him, "If this is what you're like, I want no part of you."

I slid ever so slowly into rebellion. It was just like Oswald Chambers had said, "Satan is out to shift your point of view." Satan did, and I listened.

I put God on hold, on the back burner. I didn't want him in my life. He had crushed me and deserted me in my greatest need, and I concluded that I didn't need him. I was going to be okay on my own, thank you very much.

But even when I wanted nothing to do with God, I thought, Elaine, you have another child to raise, and Nathan deserves a church home. So when my friend suggested we try a large, nondenominational mega-church in our area, I was skeptical, but as a family we went.

Little did I know that thousands of people at a worship service served me well. There I could get lost in the crowd. I could come and go with no accountability. No one even knew my name. I was there, but not really there. I could easily walk out early if I wanted, and no one questioned it. I was being dutiful in going to church, but I counted the ceiling tiles instead of listening. I was a nonparticipating participator, and this worked for me. After all, I didn't owe God a thing.

But my spiritual struggle intensified. I became angrier with God, more short-tempered, more jealous of my friends with healthy, successful children, anxious about Nathan, irritated with Tom, more fearful of the future. I appeared calm on the outside, but on the inside my heart was becoming hard and my anger more volatile. I languished between self-pity and self-loathing. Bitterness was now my closest friend.

A Prodigal's Step Forward

Jesus often taught in parables. One of his most memorable is the story of the lost son, the prodigal. For me, though, the parable is more about the father than the son. Here is my personal version of it:

Papa[60] lovingly provided life and all that was needed for his daughter. He, himself, evaluated it as "very good." One day, tragedy struck, as will happen in the earthly realm, and his daughter was deeply wounded. Instead of receiving the gifts Papa had to offer, she spurned his love, care and forgiveness, thinking that she was clever and sufficient enough to heal herself. *I really don't need you*, she thought. Years passed, her life went on, and Papa was patient. Little by little her life unraveled, leaving a bitter soul and a heart of stone. She knew she was spiritually starving and thought about all the previous blessings Papa had bestowed upon her. She missed his love, his comfort, his sweet kindness, and decided, "I want to go home. Today, I will bow before my

Father, who loves me." She knelt to pray, and while she was still speaking, the Spirit of Surrender opened the door to her heart, and Papa filled the huge void. "This is the day I have been waiting for," shouted Papa. "My precious daughter has returned!" And there was great rejoicing in heaven![61]

God waited for me ... waited ... and waited ... for years, until I heard the word *solace* in a sermon. That is the only word I remember hearing. It's a strange word, hardly used these days. What exactly is God's solace? I instantly knew what it meant. It's the comfort of God, the kindness and the sweetness that floods your heart when you know you are loved. I had missed the love of Papa. Solace. This single word penetrated my mind, and for the first time in years, I knew what was missing. Clarity had finally arrived.

A real danger in suicide survival is the overwhelming areas of conflict and confusion. There are so many issues to deal with. If you know the enemy, you can fight back! But part of satan's strategy was to keep my mind cluttered and my spirit agitated. The less I grasped, the easier I was to hold down in defeat.

So what happened when I left church that day? Was there an emotional outburst? No. Did I cry or pray? No. I was still the same on the outside, but on the inside something had changed. I shared that with Tom. I told him I had made a personal connection with God that morning, something that made sense to me.

So what was the next step, the second step? I didn't know.

My friend, on your personal road to healing, please remember this: It starts with a first step. Unless God chooses to give you a miraculous healing, you will start small and continue to grow. Do you think this was God's first attempt to connect with me? Probably not. But, once again, God gave me a healing opportunity, and I allowed it to penetrate my hard shell. I listened— finally listened—to his call.

A Healing Truth — In suicide survival, recognize you are in a spiritual battle.

Today

What I really attempted to do after Matthew died was to live in a vacuum. I purposefully ignored God because I didn't want to be available for such deep hurt ever again. To me, isolation was insulation. Slowly but surely, I started stripping everyone out of my life until I only had self, but I can tell you from experience, self is terribly inadequate. And not only inadequate but evil. Remember the garden of Eden? I'm as sinful as Eve. You cannot blame satan or God for everything.

For those years, I really did feel God was unnecessary in my healing process. How arrogant or ignorant could I have been? When a believer, a Christ-follower, is struggling spiritually, for whatever reason, he or she can be healed by God *only*. Please, hear me out. Yes, I benefitted from a helpful psychologist. Yes, I was on anti-depressant medication for a while. Yes, I had a faithful husband. I had help surviving. But my nagging struggle was a spiritual battle with God. *He* was the problem, or so I thought. And he knew he was the problem for me. But he waited for me until I realized my need for him.

God never forces himself on anyone. He is a gentleman. He calls. He woos. He invites. He even searches for us. But he never begs us or coerces us. God has given us freedom of choice, and sometimes we use that freedom to avoid him, blame him, judge him, and even fight against him. It's as if we are in the garden of Eden, behaving as Adam and Eve did.

I used my freedom to allow satan to feed my ego. His lie to me was: "You don't need a heavenly Father. You are intelligent and capable enough on your own. You will figure this out. After all, God was not there when you needed him. You are better off by yourself." I believed the lie.

My mindset, outlook, and attitude all became bitter. I became hard-hearted, and I got to the place where I didn't like myself anymore. I was becoming mean and spiteful, full of self-pity and arrogance. I angrily lashed out at people around me. Locked into myself, all I had left was self, and when you only have self, you have very little.

Psalm 73 describes this condition well:

> But as for me, I almost lost my footing.
>   My feet were slipping, and I was almost gone. ...
> Then I realized that my heart was bitter,
>   and I was all torn up inside. ...
> Yet I still belong to you;
>   you hold my right hand.
> You guide me with your counsel,
>   leading me to a glorious destiny.
> Whom have I in heaven but you?
>   I desire you more than anything on earth.

My health may fail, and my spirit may grow
weak,
> but God remains the strength of my heart;
> he is mine forever.[62]

———

Dear Papa, you know everything about me, even the number of hairs on my head. You know my thoughts, including the ugly ones lurking in the crevices of my mind. You are fully aware of my sin, and yet you love me. Thank you! While I was in the depth of rebellion, you waited. When I was arrogant in thought and deed, you loved me. While satan flattered me with his lies, you watched over me. I bow before you, fully surrendering all that I am today, broken and deficient. I ask for your full forgiveness of my stubbornness and pride and rebellion. I bow at the feet of Jesus, who is my Savior and Friend. Flood my heart with your love, peace, and joy. In your name I boldly ask. Amen.

8

Guilty or Not Guilty?

A Long-Ago Yesterday

1989–The Present

Does it ever go away? Does a person who lost a loved one by suicide ever live free of guilt?

Many deaths may involve guilt, especially when it involves children, spouses, parents, or someone else under your care. The most immediate reaction of the survivor is, I could have done more. I should have done more. Or conversely, I shouldn't have done that, or I shouldn't have said what I did. The 'could haves' and 'should haves' or 'should not haves' seem endless. And they usually come with feelings of guilt—a guilt that at times is obsessive and crushing and feels as if it will be with you forever. But it doesn't have to be this way.

My guilt was overwhelming when Matthew first died. It was massive, invasive, covering every aspect of his life, even his child-

hood. Why didn't I see "the signs" that I saw after his death? I seemed to find myself insufficient on every measurement. Did I feed him nutritionally? Start him in pre-school too soon? Help him too much at school or not enough? Did we insist too little on having him follow through on team sports or guitar lessons? Did we not discipline him enough or did we discipline too much? Did I not pray with him enough? Was I ever enough? Or was I sometimes too much?

You see, I told myself that I had failed at the one thing God had expected of me: to be a good mother to this precious baby boy he had given to us. I wasn't able to have children biologically, and when God miraculously blessed us with a son, we named him Matthew, "gift of God." Anyone who has struggled for years with infertility understands this. The gift was extraordinary! My purpose in life was now established. I was a mother, blessed more than I could have asked for or imagined. I felt that my life's work, motherhood, would provide the perfect outlet for my faith to flourish. In fact, my entire identity was now wound up around this baby boy!

I was a stay-at-home mom until Matthew entered fifth grade, and he went to a Christian elementary school from kindergarten through eighth grade. Tom drove the boys to school every day, and I picked them. This was our routine until the boys could drive. We worshiped God and served him through our church. Our marriage was solid, beautiful. We were normal, normal, normal.

I would never have imagined a suicide in our family. I had never known a suicide death of anyone. No one in my entire life had ever mentioned a suicide to me. I had no memory of anyone I knew or had been introduced to ever completing suicide. Of course, King Saul's and Judas Iscariot's suicides came to mind. How's that for endless guilt?

Tom was not affected by guilt as much as I was. For the past thirty years, he has faithfully reminded me, "Elaine, at every juncture, with every decision, we made the best choice we could and in the best interest of Matthew. We did the best we could with what we knew at the time." He still lovingly reminds me, "Don't 'should' on yourself."

Matthew left a letter for us, complete with these kind words: "You were the best parents I could possibly have had. I know you loved me. You never did anything wrong to me, but I always ended up hurting you." Matthew did not leave us with indictments of parental lack. But that didn't stop me from endlessly analyzing and criticizing my mothering.

After Matthew's death, I was racked with fear for years too numerous to count because I thought that some day Matthew's birth mother would contact us, and we would have to tell her, "Matthew took his own life." That alone seemed unbearable to me. Is it any wonder that I nearly drowned in my self-inflicted reservoir of guilt?

In the early 1980s, I was drawn to listen to Chuck Swindoll and his radio ministry, Insight for Living. It was my first venture outside of my rigid denominational background. I was drawn to him by his laughter and his fresh insight into biblical truths. I will never forget his "pickle" Christians description: "They look like they've been weaned in a pickle factory." So true. In fact, one summer our family drove cross-country to participate in a Swindoll Family Gathering at Mt. Hermon in California, and it was great. After Matthew died, Chuck Swindoll personally sent us a letter. It was positive and spoke in terms of Matthew being in heaven. What a joy it was to read! And what a ministry it helped perform in my life. It countered the voices of others who falsely told us that suicide is the gateway to hell, and Matthew had walked through it.

Today

The fact and feelings of guilt lead back to hell *and* redemption. Historically, guilt takes us back to the beginning, back to Eden. There, at the Fall, sin stares us in the face. And sin, while it results in judgment, also bears a gift—the beneficial side of guilt. It leads us to a need for redemption, for salvation. It leads us to the Savior, Jesus Christ.

When we pour over Genesis 3 and the account of the Fall, we find God making a spectacular announcement. He tells the serpent, " 'Because of what you have done, you will be the only animal to suffer this curse—for as long as you live, you will crawl on your stomach and eat dirt.' "[63] Yea God! Satan chose the form of a snake to deliver his message. Consequently, God forever cursed the serpent and thereby the rebellious angel empowering it. Many thousands of years later, those words of God still stand firm.

Continuing with his announcement, God says to the serpent: " 'You and this woman will hate each other; your descendants and hers will always be enemies. One of hers will strike you on the head, and you will strike him on the heel.' "[64] Eve and satan will hate each other. Her descendants, that is everyone ever born, every single person, will *always be enemies of satan*. One of her descendants is Jesus Christ—God Incarnate, who takes on flesh and is born as a baby in Bethlehem. He will strike satan on the head—a crucial blow, a crushing blow. Satan will be defeated! Oh, yes, and satan will bruise the heel of Jesus at the crucifixion. But on the third day, Jesus is raised to life, and that resurrection forever defeats sin, death, and the power of hell.

A Healing Truth — In the battle with sin and suicide, grace always wins!

My suffering friend, we are all part of that announcement as descendants of Adam and Eve. Your loved one is part of that announcement. Already here, in Eden, God is promising us an answer to sin. He has to come up with an answer because he is a just God, meaning perfect and holy, and he wants a relationship with his human creatures who are not perfect and holy. His desire is to spend eternity with his children—those who trust in the One he sent to save us—in complete holiness, goodness, and peace. How does he resolve the problem between us who are unholy and him who is holy?

God makes a loving, gracious decision.

A price had to be paid for the sinful choices we made, starting with Adam and Eve. A sacrifice had to be given to wipe out every sin, once and for all. Now, God makes a decision, recorded in the Gospel of John. Here it is in simplicity and clarity: " 'God loved the people of this world so much that he gave his only Son, so that everyone who has faith in him will have eternal life and never really die. God did not send his Son into the world to condemn its people. He sent him to save them! No one who has faith in God's Son will be condemned.' "[65] Read that last sentence again: "No one who has faith in God's Son will be condemned." Those are the words spoken by Jesus himself.

Hear these precious words from the lips of Jesus: " 'I tell you the truth, those who listen to my message and believe in God who sent me have eternal life. They will never be condemned for their sins, but they have already passed from death into life.' "[66]

If your loved one who died in suicide had faith in Jesus Christ, he or she is a saved child of God. He or she is perfect and holy because they are forgiven completely. No sin is exempt, except the sin of rejecting Jesus. The Bible is very clear about this: " 'Everyone who doesn't have faith in him [Jesus] has already been condemned for not having faith in God's only Son.' "[67] Condemnation comes through unbelief, not suicide.

So if anyone has told you that your loved one, who was a believer, is in hell, that is simply not true. Rejoice in that fact! Thank God for his gift of grace!

There are many theological names for God's amazing gift of grace, but my favorite is *justification*, which comes by faith in Christ. *Justification* is a legal term, and here is how it works in the legal system. Picture a courtroom. You are the defendant on trial for all of your wrong choices. The evidence is given as your life is reviewed by Father God, who is the presiding judge and jury. He takes the gavel and is ready to give his final verdict. Because of your sinful acts and your sinful nature, he would be fair and just in pronouncing you, the defendant, *guilty*— because you are.

But there is a shadow in the courtroom, and the darkness of the shadow slowly becomes a brilliant light. It is Jesus. He looks at you, smiles, and stands in front of you. Now the free gift of grace unfolds: Father God no longer sees your sin. It has been removed and washed away by the blood and death of Jesus Christ on the cross. Instead, Judge God sees the brilliant light of perfection, holiness, goodness, and peace in you, yes, *you*! Every wicked thought, every immoral act, every omission, every wrong choice is no longer there. It is as though you never sinned.

Judge God is satisfied with the life, death, and resurrection of his Son, Jesus Christ, as payment or justification for your sin. He picks up the Gavel of Justice and bangs it down with his verdict for you: Not guilty! With faith in Jesus Christ, you are saved from the punishment of incarceration in hell.

You are saved to start living eternal life right now with Jesus at your side and in your heart. "Now God says he will accept and acquit us—declare us 'not guilty'—if we trust Jesus Christ to take away our sins. And we all can be saved in this same way, by coming to Christ, no matter who we are or what we have been like."[68] Now that's good news! And "good news" is precisely what the term *gospel* means.

Just recently, much to my surprise, I found a letter sent to me dated February 5, 1998, from a good friend of mine. He was the principal at my first teaching job. He and his wife have been sweet, kind, and loving to us before and after Matthew's death. Here is what he wrote:

> When we were kids, we were told or got the impression that a person who took his own life had no chance of salvation because he/she had no choice to ask forgiveness. It finally dawned on me that such a premise is false. If we have to make sure we ask forgiveness for every sin before we pass on, then we don't live under grace, and the Gospel becomes Law. What about the Christian who drives fives miles over the speed limit (a sin) and is killed on impact in a car wreck? Is he doomed? No way!

To all those looking for hope and healing after a suicide loss, God's grace *always* wins. As a believer in Jesus Christ, you are engulfed and saturated in God's loving grace—*always!*

Father God, I want to thank you for sending your Son to be my Savior. I need a Savior, and I desire for Jesus to come into my heart, my mind, my life. I repent and turn toward belief. I believe that Jesus died for me and that you, Father God, raised him on Easter morning to pay for my sins. What relief it is to know forgiveness, to be loved, and to spend eternity with you. In Jesus's name, I pray. Amen.

God Knew

All along God knew Creation would never hold true;
Yet He spoke, it became—each day perfection anew.
Out of clay, created He a man; Adam was his name
Plus woman Eve to help, born from Adam's frame.

All along God knew the Garden would never last;
In it, sin conceived; from it, His children outcast.
But God had a plan for us—calling it Salvation
To involve everyone, all His future creation.

All along God knew His plan, His price, His guarantee
Would complete the task, from bondage set us free.
All along God knew, the price of sin absolutely paid,
His Son, thorn-crowned, on a brutal cross displayed.

Hung on a cursed tree, suffering slowly till death came.
Father knew the agony, rejection, and the shame.
God knew one more obstacle that Christ must
  overcome.
Death could hold no victory—hold no one ransom.

God planned a fabulous finish; the debt, Paid in Full!
God raised His Son—from death's grip He did pull.
What a glorious morning, an empty tomb was the place
Where God knew for certain, His plan He'd call Grace.

9

It's All My Fault

A Very Long-Ago Yesterday

Biblical Times

There once was a man named Job who lived in the land of Uz. He was blameless—a man of complete integrity. He feared God and stayed away from evil. He had seven sons and three daughters. He owned 7,000 sheep, 3,000 camels, 500 teams of oxen, and 500 female donkeys. He also had many servants. He was, in fact, the richest person in that entire area.[69]

One day, God has a conversation with satan and gives him permission to test Job, the man who has everything. God says, " 'Do whatever you want with everything he [Job] possesses, but don't harm him physically.' "[70]

Satan, of course, takes God up on this and destroys everything Job possessed. Job is left with nothing—but questions.

His story gets even worse. In a second conversation, God says to satan, " 'All right, do with him as you please … . But spare his life.' So Satan … struck Job with terrible boils from head to foot."[71] Picture this: Job is sitting on the ash heap, in sorrow. His body is bent over, disfigured, and in deep pain. Open, infected sores cover his entire body—his scalp, face, and down to the bottom of his feet. No matter how he positions himself, he is hurting. Imagine what he looks like and smells like, with flies hovering and pus oozing. He's reduced to a helpless, penniless outcast, alone, abandoned. Even his wife says to him, " 'Curse God and die.' "[72]

Why me, God? Why me? The inevitable question. Before Job even gets to ask it, three of his friends come to visit. In thirty chapters of the book of Job, they speak, one at a time. Each one blames Job for his problems and his subsequent suffering. Each so-called friend makes it clear that what happened to Job was his fault. It was all due to his sin, his own wrongdoing. They argued that Job was guilty in God's court; therefore, God was punishing him.

Job denies their accusations. He knows all too well that he is innocent of their charges and has done nothing to deserve such a severe punishment. After endless conversations and repeated accusations, Job still doesn't understand why he was going through all this pain and suffering.

Here's the bottom line. Job was a terrific guy. Words used to describe him in the various biblical translations are blameless, upright, good person, careful not to do anything evil. Still, he was not sinless. "As the Scriptures say, 'No one is righteous—not even one. No one is truly wise; no one is seeking God. All have turned away; all have become useless. No one does good, not a single one.' "[73]

Because Job is not truly wise, he demands an audience with God. He's got questions. He wants answers. From God himself.

Then God shows up in full force! God speaks to Job out of a storm. Can you imagine looking up into thick, black, towering, storm clouds, with lightning flashing, rain beating, wind howling, and a voice—*the voice of God*—thundering toward you? With bone-chilling fear griping his very soul, God asks Job, " 'Who is this that questions my wisdom with such ignorant words? Brace yourself like a man, because I have some questions for you, and you must answer them.' "[74] And God pounds Job with sixty-eight powerful questions!

A Healing Truth — God is always in control of his entire creation.

A Long-Ago Yesterday

1989–1990

In suicide recovery, there is always blame, and I had no shortage of blame for many years. For a start, I blamed Matthew's doctors. Immediately after his death, we consulted with the latest round of therapists and psychologists to let them know that Matthew had died by his own hand. You see, Matthew had turned eighteen, less than four months before his death. Consequently, we, as parents, had no right to see and hear what was in his medical file and the plan of treatment since he was now considered an adult. Sadly, now they would open his file; now, they would talk to us; now, after Matthew was dead.

Matthew had stopped going to his therapy appointments, and we could not convince him to go back. Starting six weeks prior to his death, Tom called the team of therapists and doctors numerous times and begged them to hospitalize Matthew. We knew, as his parents, that he was in a dangerous place, making bad choice after bad choice. Matthew needed help, and we knew that.

Unfortunately, you cannot hospitalize anyone against their will once they reach the magic age of eighteen unless you have proof that they intend to harm others or themselves. The doctors did not heed Tom's desperate calls for help, and time ran out. We even contacted our attorney to begin the necessary paperwork to have Matthew admitted, but time ran out. I blamed the doctors, the attorney, the system.

Of course, I also blamed some of Matthew's friends and acquaintances, especially the person who introduced him to illegal drugs. I also remembered how mean Matthew's eighth grade teacher was, and I vehemently blamed her. Sometimes I blamed Tom. Sometimes I blamed our parenting style. Sometimes I blamed our church and Matthew's school. But most of all, I blamed God and myself.

Today

Interestingly enough, I never blamed Matthew. But the truth is, Matthew made a wrong choice regardless of why the choice was made, and I may never know why he made it until I am in heaven. Perhaps then, God, the keeper of secrets, will share with me the complete answer as to why.

Which takes us back to my friend, Oswald Chambers. In the June 3rd devotion in his book *My Utmost for His Highest*, he shared this precious verse from Psalm 25:14, "The secret of the LORD is with those who fear Him."[75] He brought to my attention a very important detail about God:

> What is the sign of a friend? Is it that he tells you his secret sorrows? No, it is that he tells you his secret joys. Many people will confide their secret sorrows to you, but the final mark of intimacy is when they share their secret joys with you. Have we ever let God tell us any of his joys? Or are we continually telling God our secrets, leaving Him no time to talk to us? At the beginning of our Christian life, we are full of requests to God. But then we find that God wants to get us into an intimate relationship with Himself—to get us in touch with his purpose.[76]

The first time I really understood those words, it was 3:00 a.m., and it was many years ago. I wept through my reading of every word. Then I bowed my head and asked God for one of his secret joys, and his answer was, "Yes, Matthew is here with me."

"Father God, I thank you that you have me in the place you want me to be just now … that even if I got here through wrong choices or indifference or even rebellion, you knew my mistakes and sins before I ever existed, and you worked them into your plan to draw me to yourself, to mold and bless me, and to bless others through me.

Thank you that, even if I'm here through the ill will or poor judgment of other people, all is well; for in your sovereign wisdom, you are at work to bring about good results from all those past decisions and events beyond my control—good results both for me and for others."[77] Thank you, sweet Jesus. Amen.

10

My Grieving
Seems Like Forever

A Long-Ago Yesterday

1990–1999

   *In my grieving process, I made two huge mistakes based on what
I thought I knew. Tears often brought terrible sadness for me, and they
made others around me feel uncomfortable and awkward. So in the
best interest of everyone, I forced myself to stop crying—first bad choice.*

   *I thought lack of tears would be a positive. I always was the Pol-
lyanna of the family. In fact, Matthew often accused me of "wearing
rose-colored glasses." Yes, I did continue to cry occasionally, but it
was always in the shower or in the car when I was all by myself.
Generally, if sad moments came, I resisted them. If tears welled up
in my eyes, I turned my head so that no one could see, and I quickly*

brushed them away. At first, it was difficult to do, but soon, very soon, I became an expert at deception.

Sometime in that second year after Matthew's death, I made the second bad choice. This one came even easier. Long before I could understand, my mom and dad called me Sarah Bernhardt because I loved acting. My mother was the life of every party. So it was easy for me to make people laugh. As an adult, I often referred to myself as the Queen of Foolishness. This led to my second mistake: I found it easy and acceptable to everyone—my family, my friends, and even myself—to put on a mask. I stuffed all my feelings inside. All the pain, sadness, and struggle were pushed deep into a reservoir marked "Off-Limits. Do Not Touch." I covered up my unhappiness and hurt by putting on my happy mask.

Today

Eventually, my dear friend, if you want to get well, you *will have to touch those pain-filled feelings.* Seventeen years later, at a Christian women's retreat, Susan Dravecky taught me about grieving. Dave Dravecky, her husband, a successful San Francisco Giants baseball pitcher, lost his pitching arm due to cancer, all in the same year that both of Susan's parents passed away. She stuffed everything inside. She thought her life was over, and peace would elude her forever, and she admitted she was wrong.

A Healing Truth — In the suicide struggle, don't rely on what you think you know.

This simple truth actually comes from God's Word. It's a proverb, written by Solomon, the son of King David. Proverbs 3:5

says it this way: "Trust in the LORD with all your heart; do not depend on your own understanding." But listen to it again in the Good News Translation: "Trust in the LORD with all your heart. *Never rely on what you think you know.*"[78] Why? Because it is not always right, correct, or truthful.

The Trouble with My Way

Let's return to the book of Genesis, but not to Adam and Eve this time. Let's focus on Abram and Sarai. God tells this couple that they will be the father and mother of the entire Hebrew nation. Yes, they will have a son, and their descendants will be as numerous as the stars in the sky. The only problem from a human perspective was they were both well past childbearing years, and they had no children at that present time. Plus, God did not give them any details, such as when and how this incredible event would take place.

So Sarai starts thinking. And she thinks up a plan that sounds reasonable within the framework of the culture she lived in. Her handmaiden, an Egyptian girl named Hagar, could be the surrogate mother. Sarai tells Abram to go sleep with Hagar, reasoning, "perhaps I can build a family through her."[79] Abram thinks for a moment and then agrees with Sarai. Does this husband-wife interaction have a familiar ring? One spouse presents the other with an unwise action, and the other one agrees to it. Shades of Adam and Eve.

A baby is conceived, and Hagar, the surrogate mother, despises Sarai. In return, Sarai treats Hagar cruelly. Hagar runs away, but God knows exactly where she is and sends the angel of the LORD to tell her that she must return home, but not without a blessing: " 'I will give you more descendants than you can count,' " God tells her.[80] So Abram, who we now call Abraham, is also the father of Hagar's child, Ishmael, and the Arab nation is born.

Did Sarai's plan work? No.

Did it cause problems immediately? Yes.

Has it caused problems throughout the ages? Yes. We are *still* in conflict over the land possessed by the Jews and Arabs.

Did God have a better plan? Undeniably, yes.

How does all of this pertain to you and your struggle today?

Grieving through a suicide, without God, is like trying to fix your world through the way *you* think. It will never happen. You will never be successful on your own. Suicide grieving always involves a spiritual struggle with God because life and death are uniquely in his domain. After any death, grieving is not easy, and it provides in its path ample room for spiritual conflict. Now anytime there is a spiritual battle, satan is on the scene, and he is fighting against you through deceit, accusations, and outright lies. He will tempt you; he will twist Bible passages; he will keep the truth from you and even make you sick. But God is more powerful than satan!

Here is the huge mistake I made: I thought I knew it all, especially in the area of religion. I knew all about God, just like the Pharisees in Jesus's time. Like a tea bag, I was steeped in the dreadful sin of pride. Not only did satan lie to me and twist the truth, but I lied to myself and was content to do that. Before Matthew's death, I thought God would surely bless my efforts to faithfully follow him, not based on grace, but on my great spiritual accomplishments, high standards, and moral excellence. I thought too highly of myself. As my mentor, Oswald Chambers, succinctly states, "The greatest curse in our spiritual life is pride."[81] Until Matthew's death, I am sad to say, my life was run pridefully according to Elaine's plan: "I can. I will. I have accomplished all according to my expectations. So bless me, God."

Why Not Me?

Let me ask you a question my psychologist asked me after I wallowed in the why question. He said to me, "Why *not* you, Elaine?"

I just looked at him, amazed, rather stunned. Me? I had to answer the question, and I saw the arrogance of my pride.

Who am I to think I should never suffer?

Why should I be exempt from loss, heartache, and pain?

For centuries before me, mothers have grieved the loss of their children. Hundreds of thousands have grieved a suicide loss. So why not me too?

So let me ask you. Why not *you*?

And since you and I are not exempt, how should we handle the tragedy that has come into our lives? The early church leader James counsels us with words that I often struggle with: "Dear brothers and sisters, when troubles of any kind come your way, consider it an opportunity for great joy. For you know that when your faith is tested, your endurance has a chance to grow."[82] Joy? Are you kidding? I came, however, to understand James's words only after I had "a chance to grow" in my healing, both emotionally and spiritually. God, in his infinite wisdom, loved me through the grieving process with all of my poor choices and misguided mistakes. It was not an easy journey, and it didn't flow smoothly or quickly. But eventually—yes, after many years—it did have a positive outcome. I endured it. I grew through it.

Grieving after a suicide loss is difficult, intense, complicated, and a very slow process. It will only happen in a beneficial way when you grieve with Jesus Christ at your side and in your heart. So, where are you in the grieving process? Is Jesus your partner? Or is he the brunt of your anger?

Here is how I think grieving progresses after a suicide:

1. You are numb in disbelief and despair immediately after the death of your loved one. After the funeral, you isolate yourself at home, unable, immobile, overwhelmed.

2. Eventually, you begin to function again within the framework of family, home, and job. You are functioning in a somewhat "new normal," but you often resist the grieving process. While trying to cope, feelings get submerged. Tears are repressed. Issues do not always get worked out or resolved fully. This is where survivors often get stuck. Ask God to help you through this difficult and dangerous time. God says many times, "Fear not." He never says, "Weep not."

3. You eventually get to the point where you will begin to resolve the relationships in your life. You have personal relationships to mend with spouses, family, friends, and co-workers. Plus you are confronted with all of your emotions. But slowly, the healing takes place, and you begin to see a difference in your life. This phase may last for years, but suicide healing is always a long process. That is why you need endurance and perseverance.

4. Ultimately, your intense grief will leave emotional scars. Look upon them as your signs of success. Share them. Be proud of them. You've earned them.

As you well know, your grief struggle is present from day one, but rejoice: God is at your side and in your heart, and you *will* have joy in your life once again. But the choice is yours.

———

Oh, God, I am a mess today. I thought I was moving forward. There were joy and laughter for a change, but today I am back in the pit. This struggle is terrible! I hurt. I ache. I miss _____ so much. There are so many people who need me, and I am weary. Yes, I am weary and discouraged, and I feel like I am all alone. Help me, heavenly Father! Help me! I need strength. I need encouragement. I need you! Just let your love flow through me, sweet Jesus, and send your Holy Spirit to give me inner strength. "I can do everything through Christ, who gives me strength."[83] I will repeat that over and over because I know it to be truth, and the truth sets me free. I love you and know you are here with me. In Jesus's powerful name, I pray. Amen.

11

I'm Not Enough.
I Failed—Again.

Rejection is painful for me. Oh, I have healed considerably, but rejection lingers occasionally on the edges of my heart.

My precious son, whom I cared for and loved, rejected me, or so I thought. As a mother, it hurts deeply to be rejected by your own child, and I would think the same is true in the suicide loss of a spouse or a parent. In my experience, rejection is the deepest pain, and it lasts the longest.

Through the very act of suicide, we survivors impose rejection upon ourselves, and it comes easily. Why is that? I believe rejection actually seems logical at the time. In a sudden death, you examine the circumstances, and you make a quick decision—*I must have been part of the problem.*

But in reality, I do not know the motives that drove Matthew to his death. That's the big why question, and God hasn't shared the answer with me yet. You also may not exactly know the thoughts and motives of your loved one's mind and heart. When I was going through my season of intense depression (see chapter 2), I thought I would be helping the situation if I left. Had I done that, my husband Tom would think his wife rejected him, and my son Nathan would think his mother rejected him. But that wouldn't have been true. My thought process did not include the idea of leaving them as a way of showing them that I didn't care about them or even hated them. If I had left, my thought would have been that my departure would actually help them and maybe even me.

Remember, you are in a battle. The world around you will wag the shameful finger of rejection right in your face. Satan will easily lure you into his wrongful thinking, and we march to his step so easily. We listen quickly to his voice of deception and then repeat it over and over again to ourselves: "I am not enough. I failed again. I'm worthy of rejection. I never seem to measure up."

But, my dear friend, who is holding the standard that shows how well we measure up?

A Healing Truth— God thinks you and I are wonderfully made because he created us in his image.

I have discovered a startling piece of Scripture in the Psalms. It is startling in the respect that *if* this is truth, then at least divine rejection never plays a part in suicide. As you read this, do it prayerfully. Ask God to open your heart and mind to see the picture painted here. It's all about you and your loved one:

> You [God] made all the delicate, inner parts of my body and knit them together in my mother's womb. Thank you for making me so wonderfully complex! It is amazing to think about. Your workmanship is marvelous—and how well I know it. You were there while I was being formed in utter seclusion! You saw me before I was born and scheduled each day of my life before I began to breathe. Every day was recorded in your book![84]

As you read this biblical passage, revel in the words used to describe you. Delight in the creative process by which God made us. This is how God created you and me and our loved ones. Genesis tells us, "God looked over all that he had made, and it was excellent in every way."[85] His excellence never changes because he never changes.

Now take a closer look at the last part of what the psalmist says: "You saw me before I was born and scheduled each day of my life before I began to breathe. Every day was recorded in your book!" Everyday of my life has already been known by God and recorded for all the heavenly host to see. I imagine a conversation going on years ago in heaven—something like this:

> "Oh, Gabriel, come and take a look at this newest thought of mine. Isn't she beautiful? And look at

the gifts I have already put into her mind and into her heart. She is one of my best creations ever! Oh, she won't be born for a couple of centuries, but I know her inside and out. I have written all about her in my book. Do you want to take a look? She is my precious daughter, and I already love her very much."

Gabriel will again politely respond to his Creator's vision. He has seen billions by now, but he always marvels at God's creative genius.

"Oh," God continues, "did I mention her name is Elaine—Elaine Marie? Do I have a lifetime of action for her!"

Then God pauses and lovingly says, "Oh, Gabriel, do you see all her suffering? You know, it will accomplish my purposes for her."

Now smiling, he finishes with these words: "She'll also get a new name ... hmmm ... she gets to pick that one. Oh, you will love everything about her. I already do."

God's creativity inside me allows my imagination to picture this heavenly conversation, but I do believe this word-picture to be true. God never thinks of me as "Not Enough." God never thinks of me as "A Failure." He never stamps me "Rejected." Instead, he calls me "Daughter." You and I both, as his children, are described as "God's masterpiece."[86]

Jesus is the ultimate "Rejected One." Remember when we talked about Jesus understanding our sorrow? Well, he completely understands our feelings of rejection also. There was no room for him on the day he arrived on Earth. As a toddler, King Herod wanted him dead. The community where he grew up thought he was just a carpenter. Even family members did not believe him, not for a while. The church leaders almost completely rejected him and his miracles. The church hierarchy launched a premeditated murder plot and carried it to completion. During the last two days of his life, Jesus was betrayed, deserted, and denied by his closest friends. The Roman government caved in to a manipulated Jewish crowd, and Jesus was hung on a cross to die without mercy.

It appeared as if everyone had rejected him, even his heavenly Father. But it was all part of God's plan and purpose, faithfully announced in the garden of Eden and recorded in his book before the creation process even began.[87]

Here is something else that warms my heart: Jesus did not reject sinners. To the contrary, he was drawn to the likes of tax collectors, prostitutes, lepers, those with demons haunting them, and those who doubted. He knew all about Judas Iscariot before he ever chose him to be a disciple. When asked why Jesus ate meals with " 'such scum,' " he answered, " 'Healthy people don't need a doctor—sick people do. ... I have come to call not those who think they are righteous, but those who know they are sinners.' "[88]

His strongest words of criticism were directed toward the scribes and Pharisees, some of the religious leaders of his day. He called them white-washed tombs, hypocrites, blind fools, snakes, sons of vipers, filled with hypocrisy, and he told them that sorrow would come to them.[89]

Yes, my son Matthew was a sinner and so am I, but Jesus calls me and invites me to be in the kingdom of God as one member of the family of believers. I am God's daughter, and Matthew is his son. Both of us are sick, but both of us are healed forever. I know Matthew did not reject me, nor do I reject him. He's still my son, and I am still his mom. And more importantly still, both of us are still part of God's family and forever will be through his Son, Jesus.

———

Oh, Father God, I am humbled and awed by your love for me, which started before "I began to breathe." You knew me and created me to be your precious child for all eternity, and you did the same for _____. I will never completely understand your plan for my life or for my loved one's life, but I do understand your love for me. You proved it on the cross and at the tomb, and I am forever grateful. You, the Rejected One, never reject me. You never think of me as "Not Enough," for in Christ I am "More Than Enough." In Christ, I am fully redeemed, saved, forgiven, perfect. Thank you for healing _____. Thank you for healing me. In Jesus's beautiful name, I pray. Amen.

A Daughter of the King

God made me His precious daughter; I'm beautiful in His sight.
How wonderful are His thoughts of me. I am His pure delight.

He made me very special; there is only one of me.
His workmanship is flawless. I'm a wonder—He agrees!

Knowing me as His daughter, I'm recorded in His book.
My path of grace has been set. I believe ... that's all it took.

He loves me, cares for me, through day and nighttime too.
His peace always stays with me. His Presence I pursue.

He thinks of me, I think of Him; His love is given so free.
King of kings, Lord of lords shares Himself with little me.

God invites me to participate in His nature so divine.
He offers power through His promises, all are fully mine.

Oh, my soul, do not be cast down; do not fear or be dismayed.
The God of all creation loves and lives in me today!

12

Judged and Shunned

Stigma is when you are perceived by others to have been a part of a shameful act. You are not the harlot or the murderer, but because of your circumstances or experiences, you deserve the shame. It is shame by association, and judgment always precedes stigma. You cannot perceive others to be unworthy of respect until after you have declared them guilty. I often felt that women, especially in my age group, found me guilty by association. After all, isn't a mother directly responsible for shaping her child's thoughts and values? A mother of a suicide *has to be part of the problem!* It is through that thinking that stigma rears its ugly head.

Yet, I find it interesting that tolerance has become the norm in our society today. We tolerate every sin imaginable, and political correctness is paramount. So why are people still stigmatized by suicide? I think I know. It has a name: "The Church through the Ages." The stigma of suicide has a way of perpetuating, century after century, generation after generation.

The Church through the Ages has continually used Judas Iscariot, a disciple of Jesus, as an example. Yes, Judas was a sinner, that is for sure. We know he was a thief since he stole money out of the funds that Jesus and his disciples lived on.[90] We also know that he went to the religious leaders in secret and plotted with them to arrest Jesus.[91] We know, too, on that Thursday night when Jesus was arrested by the temple guards, as directed by the church leaders, that Judas does the unthinkable and betrays Jesus with a kiss,[92] the sign of love and friendship. All of these actions are reprehensible. But please notice the words Jesus uses in response to Judas: "My friend, go ahead and do what you have come for."[93] Jesus calls Judas his friend!

Judas did not cause the death of Jesus Christ. Sin and satan caused the death of Jesus. In fact, it was my sin and your sin and the sin of all people, including Judas's, that caused Jesus's death. The disciple, Matthew, records this important fact that God wanted us to know: "When Judas, who had betrayed him, realized that Jesus had been condemned to die, he was filled with remorse. So he took the thirty pieces of silver back to the leading priests and the elders. 'I have sinned,' he declared, 'for I have betrayed an innocent man.' "[94] Judas recognizes his sin and confesses. Then he takes his own life.

We are still left with questions as with any death by suicide. Is Judas in heaven or hell? Only God knows, for only God judges a person's heart, mind, and faith. Only God knows for sure the destination of every soul who ever lived.

I do know that if I can be given the gift of grace, so can Judas. All believers are forgiven through the life, death, and resurrection of Jesus Christ. "God saved you by his grace when you believed. And you can't take credit for this; it is a gift from God."[95] There is nothing we do to earn this salvation, nothing we can pay to buy it, and certainly nothing we have done to *deserve* it.

The Scriptures tell us, "Anyone who trusts in [Jesus] will never be disgraced." Other translations say, "will not be put to shame."[96] Two verses later, the Bible states clearly, "For 'Everyone who calls on the name of the LORD will be saved.' "[97]

So the million dollar question for you, my friend, is this: Did your loved one ever call on the name of the Lord ... on the name of God ... on the name of Jesus? Because we cannot ask them, no one living here on earth knows for sure. No one can determine what went through the mind and heart of our deceased loved ones. No one other than God can. And he makes it clear in his Word that grace is his gift to us: it always wins, it always prevails, it always dominates. Grace is given as God desires to give it, as a gift available to every person he has ever created or will create. His grace-gift rules: "Now God's wonderful grace rules instead, giving us right standing with God and resulting in eternal life through Jesus Christ our Lord."[98]

Given such wonderful revelation of God's mind and heart, I would encourage you to be kind to yourself. Remove the stigma and disgrace of suicide from your thoughts—today! Hear these kind words from gifted author, Timothy Keller: "Whatever your problem, God solves it with his grace. It doesn't matter what you have done. If you were a hundred times worse than you are, your sins would be no match for his mercy."[99]

There is no sin that escapes God's grace except the sin of saying "No thank you" to Jesus. Condemnation comes after the refusal to believe in Christ as the Savior of the world. But for "those who belong to Christ Jesus," writes Paul, "there is no condemnation."[100] And the way one comes to belong to Christ is through faith—a faith that brings with it everlasting life. As Jesus himself said, "I tell you for certain that everyone who has faith in me has eternal life."[101]

Stigma in a suicide death has often condemned the survivor as well as the deceased, but here is great news for us all. King Solomon, who was given great wisdom by God, has provided for us this perspective: "Acquitting the guilty and condemning the innocent—both are detestable to the LORD."[102]

A Healing Truth — In your battle as a suicide survivor, don't judge yourself or others; instead be kind, especially to yourself.

Beyond Judging

If you have read the New Testament, you are very familiar with Saul from the city of Tarsus, and if you have not, you can find him in the book of the Acts of the Apostles. Saul writes this interesting self-portrait in a letter he wrote to Christians in Corinth:

> As for me, it matters very little how I might be evaluated by you or by any human authority. I don't even trust my own judgment on this point. My conscience is clear, but that doesn't prove I'm

right. It is the Lord himself who will examine me and decide. So *don't make judgments about anyone ahead of time*—before the Lord returns. For he will bring our darkest secrets to light and will reveal our private motives. Then God will give to each one whatever praise is due.[103]

Here is the stunning part of this personal evaluation. Before Saul became a Christ-follower, he was a murderer, full of hatred for this Christian faith, this new brand of Jew, this paradigm shift, this new belief in a man called Jesus. Saul was a very rigid religious man and well educated in Jewish law. He searched for Christ-followers and had them imprisoned at the biding of the Jewish religious hierarchy, of which he was a staunch member. He actually approved of and physically watched while Stephen, a believer in Jesus, was unjustly stoned to death.[104]

Now, compare Saul to yourself: you haven't murdered anyone, nor imprisoned anyone, nor physically persecuted anyone for their Christian beliefs as Saul did, but you often blame yourself for your loved one's death. I know you do. And not only that—other Christians blame you too. The stigma of suicide is present, not so much by what they say but by what they don't say; not so much by what they do but by what they don't do.

In fact, Saul plainly states, "It is the Lord himself who will examine me and decide. So don't make judgments about anyone ahead of time—before the Lord returns."[105] People, sad to say, often make it their job to judge us. Sometimes they can be hurtful with intent or without it.

The tendency for others to judge suicide survivors plays out in our daily lives, including in church. After the funeral, at your church on Sunday, no one sits with you and your family in the pew, not just one Sunday but many. No one talks to you after the service. No one asks how you are doing. No one ever brings a meal. They've misjudged you and found you guilty. You are now worthy to be shunned, outcast, lonely. That's how it played out for me. And I know many other survivors who have had similar experiences.

I'm sure each one of us has had a shunning moment. Has anyone crossed the street to avoid you walking on the sidewalk? Has anyone avoided meeting you because they feel uncomfortable with your loss? Does your church avoid asking you to get involved because you just don't quite measure up? What about at the grocery store? Any sudden turnarounds in your aisle?

Remember, God is good at changing people. About two thousand years ago, he took Saul, a bigot, a hater, and a violent man, and changed him. First, God gave him a new heart with Jesus inside. Then God gave him a new mind filled with the Holy Spirit. Then God gave him a new mission: to tell others about redemption through Jesus and how to live the Christian life. Then God gave him a new name: Paul. Paul has, through the power of the Spirit of God, penned at least thirteen books of the New Testament, and he went on to become the greatest Christian missionary of the early church.

Listen to what Paul has to say about people, whether they are living or dead:

If we live, it's to honor the Lord. And if we die,
it's to honor the Lord. So whether we live or die, we

belong to the Lord. Christ died and rose again for this very purpose—to be Lord both of the living and of the dead. So why do you condemn another believer? Why do you look down on another believer? Remember, we will all stand before the judgment seat of God ... Yes, each of us will give a personal account to God. So let's stop condemning each other.[106]

It is my hope that the Christian church, through compassion and mercy, will speak out in behalf of families suffering a suicide loss, not condemning them but comforting them and helping them to heal. The stigma is there, and we dare not pretend it isn't. But fellow Christians can remove it by responding with compassion and understanding—in other words, by living out God's healing grace.

Gracious heavenly Father, forgive those who know you and believe in you, yet misjudge and find others lacking. Even many pastors and priests are sometimes hesitant to talk about suicide and the spiritual battle involved in addictions and mental illness. Help us all to accept those who suffer, who are hurting through no fault of their own. Forgive the church through the ages for the sins committed in the name of Jesus, and we know that grace covers that too. Today I desire to move forward with the power of Jesus in my mind and heart. Help me! Provide all that I need, one day at a time. I am stepping out in faith, knowing that you love me, and I am trusting you to lead me. I ask in the name of my Savior. Amen.

PART THREE
HOPE AND HEALING

I will never forget this awful time, as I grieve over my loss. Yet I
still dare to hope when I remember this: The faithful love of the
Lord never ends! His mercies never cease. Great is his faithfulness; his mercies begin afresh each morning. I say to myself,
"The Lord is my inheritance; therefore, I will hope in him!"

Lamentations 3:20–24

Congratulations—you got this far!

Earthly time is our dimension, not God's. The Bible tells us
that "a day is like a thousand years to the Lord, and a thousand
years is like a day."[107] He created light and darkness to mark a
solar day, twenty-four hours. He knew our limitations; in fact,
he created us with limitations and provided boundaries to pro-

tect us. Twenty-four-hours is one of those boundaries. Today is all we have. No one on planet Earth has more or less. Time is the great equalizer of us all.

So let's celebrate the gift of an unrepeatable day—today!

Let's also celebrate our uncommon commonality, having gone through the death and suffering of a suicide.

Let's celebrate that we are now looking forward with hope. Ahh, not only looking forward but moving forward. That is my desire. Come with me. Make an intentional decision to move forward with the help of God. No matter where you are in your battle, it will help you to think forward.

Tell someone you know about your decision—that's important. Of course, start by talking with God, and daily ask for his power to provide all you need, one day at a time. This is not a do-it-yourself project. You desperately need God's help, but it is not a team sport either. You and God together make up the perfect pair.

———

Oh, Father God, here I am, making an intentional decision to move forward in my journey of grief. I cannot do it on my own, but with your help I can heal. Some days I am overwhelmed and powerless. Some nights I am fearful and anxious. Flush out my anger and resentments, my guilt and self-pity. Flood me with your love, and clothe me in a robe of righteousness,[108] all for the sake of Jesus, my Redeemer and Friend. Amen.

13

I Need to Talk to You, Papa

"God takes us to places we never imagined we would be." I had scribbled those words in a notebook some time ago, and I saw them again just recently. I stopped in my tracks and thought, *Hey, that's me.* I laughed when I saw that I had applied them to Jonah. I really do believe God has a sense of humor. But here's the really funny part—it *is* me. I am very similar to that ancient prophet.

Jonah makes some very poor choices, but God uses him anyway. God sends him on a very important mission: " 'Up on your feet and on your way to the big city of Nineveh! Preach to them. They're in a bad way and I can't ignore it any longer.' " The next verse is quite startling: "But Jonah got up and went the other direction ... running away from God. He went down to the port of Joppa and found a ship headed for Tarshish. He paid the fare and went on board, joining those going to Tarshish—

as far away from God as he could get."[109] He definitely ignores God. He blatantly resists God's assignment for him.

God's response matches Jonah's audacity: God sends a huge storm exactly where the ship is traveling, and through an interesting process, Jonah is thrown overboard. Immediately the storm stops. God's power and providence are on display! He provides for a great fish or sea creature of some kind to swallow Jonah. He masterfully takes the disobedient prophet to a place he never imagined he would be.

"Then Jonah prayed to his God from the belly of the fish."[110] I bet he did.

Today, you are a Jonah. I am a Jonah. God has taken us to a place we never imagined we would be.

Have you prayed to God recently? Or are you too afraid to pray? Or are you too angry or cynical to pray? You might even wonder what difference prayer makes anyway. What good is it?

In my battle, here is what I said to God: "Okay, God (jabbing my finger into his chest). Do you even *remember* me? (Cynicism.) I *did* pray, trusting and believing everything I said to you. (Anger.) I even thanked you before you would answer. Now my son is *dead*! Obviously, prayer *doesn't* work *that* way. (Screaming.) You know what? I don't *know* how prayer works! (Seething.) I don't know how *you* work, so I'm done." And I was.

Silence. A long silence, months of silence, years of silence. Through it, I learned something about God. Silence doesn't bother him. No, in fact, God is very good at silence. He waited, and he waited some more, and he may be waiting for you right now.

Here is some sage advice: tell God *everything*! Yes, right now, spill your guts. Scream, shout, whisper, cry, sob, fume, shake your fist, gloat, use sarcasm, be cynical, laugh, sneer, belittle him, be terrified of him, say stupid things, jump up and down, fall to your knees. Just don't ignore him. Because God knows exactly what you are feeling and thinking anyway. He knows you inside and out. In fact, God knows everything. So you might as well tell him, and that, my friend, *is* prayer.

Prayer is talking to God, and talking is where all relationships begin. Today, right now, within your anger or your disappointment or your sorrow, repair your relationship with God. Put aside your pride and your sulking and restore your relationship with him.

A Healing Truth—You will never resolve your conflict with God by ignoring him. Prayer draws you closer to him.

Suffering has a purpose. Through trials, we learn obedience; we gain endurance; our faith is strengthened; perseverance increases. Is it any wonder, then, that God allows suffering in the lives of his children? Yet so many well-meaning Christians think of God as the great "Vending Machine in the Sky." If you pray, and get all your friends to pray, and you push all the right buttons, out pops your blessing.

We often hear comments like this: "Praise God, our prayers were answered, and the cancer was healed. God is good." The prayers went into the vending machine and out popped the favored answer. Therefore, God is good. Right? Let me ask you: Is God only "good" when he says yes? Is he only good when we get what we want or even better? If so, is God then "bad" when he says no, when he doesn't deliver the answer we so desire to receive?

Just recently, I heard a well-meaning Christian say these exact words in relationship to prayer: "I believe good things happen to good people." That thought is simply not true. All prayers get answered all the time: some yes, some no, some wait. And the answer is God's decision, not ours. As King of kings and Lord of lords, God rules over all of his creation. He provides healing, but not because the one who prayed is good. Good people don't get only "good" and bad people don't get only "bad."

Remember when Jesus and his disciples met a blind man, they asked Jesus, " 'Who sinned, this man or his parents, that he was born blind?' " Jesus answered, " 'Neither this man nor his parents sinned, … but this happened so that the words of God might be displayed in him.' "[111] God decided in his sovereignty to display his mighty healing hand, and Jesus healed the blind man, no matter how good or bad his parents were, or how good or bad his friends were, or how many prayers were spoken on the blind man's behalf. The benefit of prayer is that it surrenders our desires to God's sovereignty and our weaknesses to his strengths. For me, prayer is the perfect pairing, the perfect combination: God's strength with my weakness.

So as you become more proficient and comfortable with talking to God and loving him back, you can also learn how to listen to him. After all, when you talk, God listens. Give him the same courtesy. I was tutored by Sarah Young through her amazing book, *Jesus Calling*. Very slowly I started hearing what Jesus had been saying for years: "I love you, Elaine. I love you, Elaine," and he had to say it over and over and over again.

In January 2013, I started spending time each day journaling what Jesus said to me. My mother had just died. A few days later, I went through my fourth knee surgery—this time a complete revision, which is a replacement of the first replacement. I was in bed, totally incapacitated and in pain, physically and emotionally. On the second day, I wrote this in my journal after I had quietly listened to God:

> "I will equip you for this day, Elaine. Look to me for everything you need. Through all the choices you make today, whisper, 'Help me Jesus. Help me Holy Spirit.' Choose me first each day, then everything else will be added. I love you, and I delight in blessing you. I have great compassion for you."

Sometimes it seems easier to talk to Jesus because he is "God with skin on." But just as you can talk directly with Jesus, you can also speak directly to the Father or the Holy Spirit or with the triune God all at once. Prayers can be short or long. They can be sung or can be thoughts. You can come to God with all of your "priors": addiction to guilt, wallowing in self-pity, berating yourself, blaming everyone, full of rage, or so despondent and drawn inwardly that you feel numb.

Jonah thought he could avoid God's call by running away. He thought he could belligerently avoid obedience to God's call. He was wrong, and God, in his ultimate wisdom, drew Jonah back into relationship.

My dear, wounded friend, I do not know why God would choose us to bear the trauma of a suicide. None of us signed up for this. None of us volunteered. But there is something inside each of us that God desires to use.

Before creation, before the garden of Eden, God knew. God knew about the struggles of our loved ones. God knew they would someday make a terrible choice, a stupid choice, a dangerous choice. But God still loved them, and he still loves you. "Love never stops being patient, never stops believing, never stops hoping, never gives up."[112]

Did God answer my prayer for the healing of Matthew two weeks before his death? For many years, I relied on what I thought I knew. I thought God did *not* heal Matthew. I thought God had clearly said no. However, God led me to the truth, as he always does. "Elaine," he said, "Yes, I healed Matthew, just not the way you expected him to be healed. He is here with me in heaven, totally healed and at peace. Well done, thou good and faithful servant."

Today, *you* write the prayer.

———

Father, I have a lot of questions …

Sweet Jesus, thank you for …

Holy Spirit, help me with …

Oh, Lord, this is how I really feel …

14

God, If You Are Love,
I Need Some

Let's go back to the prom. The simple truth God shared with me at the prom is choose life. I'm now going to revisit that message, beginning with the Hebrew leader Moses as he gives his final speech to the Hebrew nation God had created: " 'Now listen! Today I am giving you a choice between life and death, prosperity and disaster. ... Oh, that you would choose life. ... You can make this choice by loving the LORD your God, obeying him, and committing yourself firmly to him. This is the key to your life.' "[113]

Oh, yes, the message is clear and simple and even concise, but not necessarily easy to live out. Understand this before I go any further: prosperity means a rich, full life, not a wealthy bank account. For the sake of this conversation, I am labeling spiritual healing in my battle with suicide survival as *the* prosperity. Yes,

I have had other blessings, but for me, spiritual healing was the ultimate blessing. Once I started to believe that God loved me, my spiritual healing started.

The first ten years of life after Matthew's death were the most difficult, and I am happy to share that I was healed by the power of the Holy Spirit working in me, even though I was stubborn and rebellious. It happened by the grace of God. About halfway through those ten years, my husband and I joined a nondenominational megachurch, and for the first time, we were in a place where healing could begin. People were kind, loving, and accepting of us. Plus, we met many other hurting people. Misery *does* love company. I didn't feel so alone.

A major breakthrough came in the fall of 1996 when we met Pastor Ron Dunn, who came to speak at the Mission Festival at our church. We always sat in the church balcony, and I really didn't even want to go to this extra church service on a Sunday night, but for some reason, we did. "And it came to pass," God put us in the third row from the front, right in line with the speaker. I wanted to just sit there and count the ceiling tiles, tuning out what was going on around me, but then our pastor introduced the speaker as a "man who knew great pain." I actually listened. He never used the word *suicide*, but I knew in my heart what his struggle and pain was. I felt a connection.

Our church had its own bookstore, and after the service, I bought the speaker's book, *When Heaven Is Silent,* and read every word that night. It was as though God dropped a huge gift right into my heart. Pastor Dunn's eighteen-year-old son had taken his own life. Their family's experience was our family's experience. Excitedly, Tom and I arranged to meet with

Pastor Dunn the next evening. The three of us talked, we shared, and we prayed, and I vividly remember this one sentence: "Trust me, you *will* have joy again in your life." Pastor Dunn was adamant, I believed him, and I hung on to that kernel of truth tightly.

A Healing Truth — Always remember, God loves you, and shows his love in many ways.

I did not feel loved by God for a very long time. I think most of you would say that you haven't felt loved by God either, at least not for some time. I *knew*, as with informative knowledge, that God loved me because I *knew* John 3:16. I *knew* in my mind that the greatest love for me was manifested by Jesus Christ on the cross and in his resurrection from the tomb. But I didn't *feel* God's love. Why? Because I hadn't realized what his love really is. The essence of God's love is joy. His love is not ordinary love, nor is it ordinary joy. It is God's supernatural love demonstrated and revealed through its essence, joy.

Ron Dunn was God's messenger to Tom and me, and I want to be God's messenger to you. You will have joy again in your life. Real joy! The essence of God's love will permeate your heart once again. Hang on to that truth. Trust me, it will happen.

But there is a catch, a caveat, a condition, a caution. Your heart will have to be open to God so that his love and joy can enter. A cold, closed heart will never receive love or joy. Here's the red flag for suicide survivors: We think we do not deserve God's love and joy. Guilt, blame, and negative self-talk says, "I will never be joyful again because *I deserve misery. I am unlovable.*"

You may think like that. I know I did. But this awful message is not true. God does not desire for you to languish in painful misery. He led me to this beautiful verse: "Therefore God, your God, has set you above your companions by anointing you with the oil of joy."[114] It's actually a part of a wedding song, but I made that verse mine. In the margin of my Bible, I have this tag, "Dec. 1999 — Me!"

That exact verse is again quoted in the New Testament book of Hebrews in chapter one, verse nine. This time it refers to Jesus. In Hebrews, this conversation takes place: God the Father is talking to God the Son and says, " 'You love justice and hate evil. Therefore, O God, your God has anointed you, pouring out the oil of joy on you more than on anyone else." God the Father pours out the oil of joy on God the Son more than on anyone else.' " Then Jesus pours that oil on us!

Daily I pictured God's oil flowing over my head and down my body. I pictured it running into my heart and down into the snarls of my soul, untangling all the hurts I had hung on to. I felt it soothing the ripples of pain in my mind, erasing the rebellion, and slowly changing my bitter heart. For me, there was no instant miracle, no sudden shift, just God's unfailing love, penetrating my pain. Like the drip, the constant drip of water eroding stone, God's joy eroded my hard heart.

Yes, that "drip of joy" changed the way I looked at myself and others. I learned this from a sweet friend of mine. I watched her interaction with total strangers: the parking lot attendant, the fast food employee, the one mopping the floor in the supermarket, the bank teller. She noticed each person and acknowledged their presence through her greeting, a smile, a brief remark, a bit of humor. She brought sunshine into their lives. Their faces lit up every time, and hers did too.

How did love and joy return to me? With baby steps, I started modeling her behavior. Instead of hurriedly walking past people, head down, brows furrowed, and a chip on my shoulder, I started noticing people around me and actually seeing them. I noticed many of them looked sad too. At first, I felt awkward, but I just smiled at them as I passed—not a big, toothy grin, just a sweet smile. And I looked them in the face. Much to my amazement, they smiled back, and their response lifted my spirit. I did that over and over and over again.

"Watch to see where God is at work, and join him" is the advice given in one of my favorite books, *Experiencing God*.[115] We tend to think God works in big events and big arenas and planned programs. But you can join God where he is working in everyday moments, in the lives of simple, hurting people like you and me. You can give joy freely, and it won't cost you a thing—a look, a smile, patience as you open a door for someone, a greeting, a nod of approval, an encouragement. And you will receive God's love and its essence, joy.

Little by little, that joy changed the way I thought, changed the way I made decisions, changed the way I looked at myself. I was not deserving of misery, absolutely not. Instead, I was buoyed by these words: "You [God] have also given me the shield of Your salvation, and Your right hand upholds and sustains me; Your gentleness [Your gracious response when I pray] makes me great."[116] Just picture the scene described in Psalm 18—God scooping you up, holding you in his arms, protecting you, saving you, sustaining you with his love. He gives you his shield of victory and then lovingly stoops down to your level to make you look great. Why? Because you *are* great! You *are* his beloved and redeemed child. He loves you with an unfailing love! "See what great love the Father has lavished on us, that we should be called children of God! And that is what we are!"[117]

Oh, gracious Papa, drip your love into my bitter heart. I open it to you here and now. I desire your love. I desire your joy. I want to feel loved, redeemed, accepted, and right with you, so I pray today for the "oil of joy" to be mine. Anoint me, loving Jesus, and change the way I think about myself. Help me to graciously accept your gift of love, just as you graciously respond to this, my heartfelt prayer. I love you, God, and thank you for loving me first, even in my stubbornness. Make me a vessel of love to others. Help me, Jesus, to smile and notice hurting people so I can be kind to them. In your name I pray. Amen.

Nothing Is Wasted

Nothing is wasted when you walk close to Me!
Not trials, they bring trust.
Not fear, it grows faith.
Not sickness, healing provides patience.
Not anger, it releases, gives rest.
Not problems, they force prayer.
Not temptation, it reaps restraint.
Not pride, it can be pruned.
Not judgment, humility is honed.
Not suffering, for when suffering is surrendered,
Joy brings Peace to the Soul.

15

What Is the Right Thing to Do Today?

My dear friends, we are bonded by our suffering and the battle we are fighting. I am an ordinary mother. I am a redeemed child of God, saved by grace because of what Jesus has done, just like you. And I am living proof that a full, happy life is possible after grieving a suicide death. The battle for this kind of life is won or lost in your mind. How you think will bring you to success or failure.

You will need mentors and companions along the way. One excellent and trustworthy mentor is Rick Warren, pastor at Saddleback Church in California and founder of the global ministry *Pastor Rick's Daily Hope*. Pastor Rick is the author of another of my favorite books, *The Purpose Driven Life*, a Christian classic. His ministry has touched my heart numerous times. Listen to what he says: "If you want to change the way you act, you start by changing the way you think. In addition, if you want to change the way you feel, you must start with the way you think."[118] And what all of us need to think on is the truth.

Right now, survivor, truth will be your best friend. The more truth you repeat to yourself, the faster you will move forward in your healing. So take this little survey. On a daily basis, ask yourself:

1. What am I watching?
2. What am I reading?
3. What am I googling?
4. What music am I listening to?
5. Who are my personal advisors, mentors, and other human sources of information?
6. Who am I spending time with?
7. What am I doing with my spare time?

Through all of these venues, are you putting truth into your mind? Are you listening to truth? Do you spend time with people who are truthful? Even if you are weary, worn out, and completely emptied, please take some time each day to read something out of your Bible. I resisted that. I thought I had a better plan, but *I was wrong.*

A Healing Truth — Obedience to God's truth will be your number one healing agent!

I learned something about obedience that was a game changer for me. I found another gem in Oswald Chamber's book *My Utmost for His Highest*. Listen to his wisdom:

> All of God's revealed truths are sealed until they
> are opened to us through obedience. And it is not
> study that brings understanding to you, but obe-
> dience. Even the smallest bit of obedience opens
> heaven, and the deepest truths of God immediately
> become yours. Yet God will never reveal more truth
> about Himself to you, until you have obeyed what
> you know already.[119]

Obedience is not about rules. It is about a relationship with almighty God.

About six hundred years before Jesus was born, the country of Israel was invaded by troops from Babylon. Their ruler, King Nebuchadnezzar, turned the government of Judah into a vassal state. He also promptly took the brightest and best of Judah's men into exile. As political prisoners, they were confined to a strict three-year training regimen to learn the language and culture of Babylon. This wasn't a student foreign-exchange program. These prisoners were part of an act of war and were subjected to Babylonian brainwashing. They ate, slept, and thought Babylon—at least that's what their captors demanded and desired of them. Even their names were changed; they were given Babylonian names to replace their Hebrew names. And among these exiles were teenagers.

One of these Hebrew teenagers, Daniel, and three of his friends found themselves in a foreign country, stripped of family, forced to adhere to strict training, and miles away from anything Jewish. They were forced to eat food and drink wine directly from the king's table. "But Daniel was determined not to defile himself by eating the food and wine given to them by the king."[120] That was Daniel's mindset. He was mentally determined not to defile himself by eating foods God had not approved. He made a gutsy decision, a dangerous decision, but he knew in his mind that it was the right thing to do, so he did it:

> He [Daniel] asked the chief of staff for permission not to eat these unacceptable foods. ... "Please test us for ten days on a diet of vegetables and water," Daniel said. "At the end of the ten days, see how we look compared to the other young men who are eating the king's food. Then make your decision in light of what you see."[121]

Before we get to the rest of the story, let's go back to what Oswald Chambers had to say: "God will never reveal more truth about himself, until you have obeyed what you already know." What did Daniel already know about God? He knew God required his people to eat only certain foods, and Daniel desired to be obedient to those requirements. The Bible says he was "determined"—that is a mental as well as an intentional decision. He did not rationalize, reason, or resist God's revealed standard for his people.

Once that decision was made, how do you think Daniel came up with his plan of action to present to the chief of staff? God gave him the plan, put it into his mind, and then waited for Daniel to act—and he did. The Bible also tells us what happened. "At the end of the ten days later, Daniel and his friends looked healthier and better nourished than the young men who had been eating the food assigned by the king."[122] Who blessed them? Who made it all happen? God did.

Just like us, Daniel found himself in a very unfair situation, one he didn't ask for. Not only that, Daniel spent the rest of his life in enemy territory, serving as a close advisor to two Babylonian kings and then two Mede/Persian kings who came to power after defeating Babylon.

Through the years, God gave Daniel great power to interpret dreams, gave him insight into deciphering strange writing on the wall, made him governor of the land, allowed him to remain alive in a den of ferocious lions, and gave him visions of the future. And all of this began with what Daniel knew about God as a very young man. Despite his circumstances, despite how he felt, Daniel made a determined decision to build on what he knew as truth and obey it.

What do you know about God today? I humbly believe, based on what I know about God, that he desires you to be in a relationship with him. Even if you are angry, perplexed, or just plain empty at the moment, what do you know about God and his expectations of you today?

Please grab a sheet of paper, your journal, or one of your electronic devices, and write down what you think God expects of you today. If you believe in Jesus Christ as your Savior, does he expect to be worshiped? Does he expect you to give something back to him as an offering? Does he desire for you to pray— before meals, at bedtime, first thing in the morning? To read his words? To show kindness to your spouse? Love your children? Work your job as best you can? Help your neighbors? What is the right thing to do today? You know what it is. Write it down.

Now, whatever you have written, do it! Your determined effort, whatever it is, will be "the smallest bit of obedience which opens heaven." That is what worked for me. It was the start, the beginning of real healing for me.

Often when I sat in the balcony with my husband and I counted the ceiling tiles, I also heard something from the sermon—something that truly impacted me. Tom brought our financial offerings to God. I sang some of the songs (only those I liked). And I read from the Psalms, between tears, sadness, anger, and blame. We also asked the Lord to bless our meals, even though Matthew was missing from around our table. We did read Ron Dunn's book. All those small actions initiated a healing start for us.

I heard the word *solace* in a sermon, remember? What did I do in response to that? I knew God wanted me to surrender my heartache to him, also my disobedience, my rebellion, and my pride. I bowed and gave everything to God in prayer that day. I confessed my sin and gave up control of my life. It was a beginning for me—a new direction, another small step. Heaven opened and God blessed. I felt God's love again, which encouraged me.

So "let God transform you into a new person by changing the way you think."[123]

Almighty God, you are the God of Daniel, and you are my heavenly Father. I believe you exist and that you love me, even if I don't always feel loved. I know that Jesus died for me, and I am your redeemed child. Help me think through what you expect of me now, today. Lead me and guide me to know you better. Then, through your power, help me be obedient to you! I am trusting you to heal me by changing the way I think. Use your truth, and may it bless me more than I can imagine. In the powerful name of Jesus, I pray. Amen.

—⁂—

If you are not in a relationship at all with God, you can start thinking like this: *God, I am hurting because of _____'s suicide. I don't know what to do, but I do know I need help of some kind, and yes, I would like you to help me. Come and help me today, even though my life is really a mess right now. I have made a lot of bad choices too, just like _____. Help me find Jesus in the Bible. My obedience in seeking you will be putting the You Version app [or some other Bible app] on my phone and reading something about Jesus from the Gospel of John or the 23rd Psalm. So help me God!*

16

The Power of
Keeping Promises

These are the keys to life according to God: love, obedience, and commitment. Regarding love, God wants you to receive his lavish love for you so you can love him back and love others around you. Concerning obedience, he wants you to obey what you know to be his truth. And when it comes to keeping promises, he wants you to commit yourself to him. These three come down to loyalty and faithfulness over the long haul.

Unfortunately, the concept of commitment is almost dead in America, whether it is in a marriage, a job, a church, or even a family. People are opting out, quitting their commitments.

When Moses gave his farewell speech, he specifically said these words: " 'I am making this covenant both with you who stand here today in the presence of the LORD our God, and also with the future generations who are not standing here today.' "[124] God declared that he would be faithful to the covenant, and he was. But would the people be faithful to it too? No, they were not.

The faithlessness of ancient Israel didn't end with them. God's people still struggle with faithfulness, even under the new covenant initiated by Jesus. And at the center of the new covenant is something that was also at the center of the old one: to love God with all we are and have and to love others even as we love ourselves.[125] I wasn't always great on loving God and others, that's for sure, and I wasn't always great at obedience with my anger and rebellion. But the one thing I did right was commitment. It happened the day I walked out on Tom. Sounds like an oxymoron, but here is what happened.

We moved out of the Lake House fourteen months after Matthew died. At first, I loved being in that house, but after awhile, I found it very depressing. No matter where I went, Matthew's presence was alive—out in the yard, down by the lake. I was always sad. I couldn't avoid it. Our sweet Old English sheepdog, Lizzie, got throat cancer during that first year of our grief, and we had to have her put down. Now, even the doghouse was empty. That entire place seemed to hold sorrow. Plus, I couldn't look at all the family pictures hanging on the walls, and the "Jonah" in me was very good at running away. So we moved.

After I hired someone to take over my retail business, I tried all sorts of odd jobs. For a school year, I was a half-day teacher at an elementary school. For another year, I was a "headhunter" at a recruitment agency. Then I applied to work for an airline company, and when they offered me a job, I decided it was too far from home, so I turned them down. Then I actually worked, instead of my own retail store, at another retail store in a large, regional mall about forty-five minutes from our house. I went back to college and worked on my master's degree. Did I mention that I was good at running away?

This was the first five years after Matthew died. What a mess I was in—our marriage wasn't doing well either. We started growing apart. I had nothing to give, and neither did Tom. We were both on empty and had been for a long time.

One day, after another argument, I walked out the front door angrily, shouting these words: "I'd rather live all by myself." I slammed the door, got into the car, and drove and drove, and thought and thought. But the good news was that by the end of the day, I returned home again. This time with an entirely different mindset.

A Healing Truth — Satan's strategy in your battle is to win the war.

Often, I think back to that car ride. What went through my mind? I was in turmoil. I didn't fit in anywhere—not at work, not at home, not with Tom, not with God. Nathan was my only ray of sunshine. He was my blessing of all blessings during this difficult time. I didn't want to lose him too.

Somewhere in all of my thoughts during that crucial car ride, this is what came to me. If I walked out now on our marriage and our family, all of those relationships would be damaged. Nathan, who had lost a brother, would now lose a close family. And who in all the world would ever understand my battle? *No one* would ever understand like Tom. I would lose my best friend. If I walked out, satan would win it all and that upset me. He had already damaged enough. I was not going to let him win the war. I resisted with all my heart and mind. I said no to satan!

It was so clear to me. Like a shot of adrenaline, I had a wake-up call. I went back home—with a firm grip on loyalty, faithfulness, and the long haul. Roughly twenty-five years later, Tom and I are still together—living in the fullness of God.

Keeping your promises never comes easily because you have to be intentional. It takes effort and work. No one can do it for you. You must work on doing it until it becomes part of the way you operate. Of course, God in his mercy helped me, but I did have something I put in front of me every day. I found a large piece of artwork, a calligraphy by artist Timothy Botts. It depicts a conversation between King David and his son, Solomon, regarding the building of God's temple in Jerusalem. This is what it says on the background in small letters: "Be strong and courageous and get to work, for the LORD, my God, is with you. He will not forsake you. He will see to it that everything is finished correctly."[126]

Then, in red and very large letters, you see these words pop out over the Bible verse: "DON'T BE FRIGHTENED BY THE SIZE OF THE TASK." Mr. Botts didn't realize it when he created this, but God had him design and make this especially for me and my task—to get through this battle of suicide survival with victory because God would see to it that everything would be finished correctly.

Here is what many people do not understand: in a relationship, sometimes commitment is all you have left, but here's the kicker—that is enough! Without commitment in a relationship, you have absolutely *nothing*.

Here's how it worked for me. Even though I rebelled against God and walked away, I was still committed to him. Through my relationship with Jesus Christ, I was still a child of God. God did not disown me because I behaved the way I did. He did not deny my existence nor declare me outside of his family. Yes, he was silent, but I had asked him to leave. He still loved me through all of my mistakes. I caused the estrangement. But because of the commitment we shared, eventually our relationship was reconciled and restored.

What about my marriage to Tom? It was strained, not abusive. It was unhappy, not life-threatening. I can only speak to my situation, but if Tom and I had not been married, if we had not been committed to staying together for "better or worse," we could have easily parted. Sometimes commitment is all you have, but sometimes commitment is all you need.

Do not be frightened by your task. Get to work. Here is something written especially for you, dear friend: " 'The eyes of the LORD search the whole earth in order to strengthen those whose hearts are fully committed to him.' "[127]

Dear heavenly Father, thank you for your faithfulness to me through the years. You have always loved me. Even before I was born, you loved me, and you didn't cast me away from your presence, even if I ignored you. Thank you for your commitment to me through your son, Jesus Christ. Because of him, I am your forgiven child, and I know, without a doubt, that I will spend eternity with you. Today I promise my love, commitment, and especially my obedience to you.

Help me with all that, Spirit of God, so that when I come home to you, I will hear the words, "Well done, thou good and faithful servant." In the loving name of Jesus, I pray. Amen.

17

Forgiveness:

Your Hardest Task,
Your Greatest Reward

Dear survivor, you *are* moving forward. After all, you have stayed with me up to this chapter. There is a Bible verse that describes you today: " 'Blessed are your eyes, because they see; and your ears, because they hear.' "[128] I would also add that I think your heart is open. That's good, because this may be a difficult chapter.

You got here, in this suicide struggle, because of someone else's action. You did not sin; someone else did, and worse yet, someone you personally loved, and still worse, someone with whom you cannot communicate. Now, sin needs forgiveness. What does forgiveness look like and to whom should it apply in the context of a suicide? That's going to be our focus here.

Let's begin with getting some clarity. Who are your biggest stumbling blocks? Who do you need to forgive?

Is it your loved one—the person who died?

Or is it someone else in your family?

Is it the doctor who prescribed the narcotic?

Or the person who sold your loved one the gun?

Is it an unknown drug dealer or a failed prison system?

Is it a close friend or a number of friends?

Is it a pastor or someone within your church or even *the* church?

Or is it you?

You probably need to apply forgiveness to more than one person. Make a list. If there are many on your list, prioritize them.

Without your forgiveness of them, they will remain stumbling blocks for you. Worse—they will be links of a chain forever keeping you in bondage to your tragic loss. The prophet Isaiah paints a truthful picture for us: "What sorrow for those who drag their sins behind them with ropes made of lies, who drag wickedness behind them like a cart!"[129] Without forgiveness on your part, you will be forever dragging lies around with you, and the heaviness will never end. Call them chains, call them ropes, but they will render you unable to live freely, without guilt, blame, and sorrow. Healing will be impossible.

Of course, forgiveness will be hard to grant. How I wish that I could victoriously claim, "Yes, I forgave all my stumbling blocks easily." But I struggled ... and struggled ... for years. I hung on to lies that I believed to be truths. I got stuck in that place called "Unforgiveness." There were so many issues to address, and I had so little energy to deal with them. I hung on to all my hurts and disappointments and replayed them over and over in my head. I found it impossible to forgive because I hardened my heart and refused to change.

The number one person on my list was me. For years I berated myself, blamed myself, and held myself accountable to unattainable standards. God was patient, and he taught me a lot about myself through a book I came to love, *The Shack*, by William P. Young. It's a fictional story, but I could identify with the main character, Mack. His youngest daughter is abducted and murdered, and Mack's life is forever changed by "*The Great Sadness.*" He blames himself and God, and God shows up to prove him wrong. Eventually, Mack is healed, but it takes forgiveness.

Like Mack, do you blame yourself? Do the *what ifs* play over and over in your mind? Do you sometimes feel that you are haunted by blame because you feel somewhat responsible? Do you wonder if absolution of yourself might somehow negate your love for the deceased? Do you feel you deserve the role of martyr or perhaps even enjoy it? Do you understand that if God forgives you and you do not forgive yourself, more than self-blame is involved—you are also prideful?

A Healing Truth — Freedom comes through forgiveness. Forgiveness changes everything!

Forgiveness sets you free from horrible thoughts, from gloom and confusion, from false guilt, from being forever bound by your wrong thinking, from a miserable life.

How do you forgive all those people on your list? How do you forgive yourself? Here is your first step. Pray, "Today, Father God, I am letting go. I am unloosing the chains that have shack-

led my thoughts for so long. I am intentionally letting go of
_____." Tell God what and who you are releasing, and ask
for *his* power to help you forgive completely. You can do it—
nothing is impossible with God according to his plan and purpose. Here is what the apostle Paul had to say about *his* life: "I
know how to live on almost nothing or with everything. I have
learned the secret of living in every situation ... . For I can do
everything through Christ, who gives me strength."[130]

Does that mean healing happens instantly? No. You took a
first step; it is a beginning.

Listen to this true-life story:

> One of the men lying there [at the Pool of
> Bethesda] had been sick for thirty-eight years.
> When Jesus saw him and knew he had been ill for a
> long time, he asked him, *"Would you like to get well?"*
>
> "I can't, sir," the sick man said, "for I have no
> one to put me into the pool when the water bubbles
> up. Someone else always gets there ahead of me."
>
> Jesus told him, "Stand up, pick up your mat,
> and walk!"[131]

Let me ask you something I wish someone would have asked
me many years ago: Would you like to get well? I do not want to
be insensitive to anyone, believe me. If your family's suicide happened recently, you are still in the thick of the grieving process.
But if you are stuck, if you continue to berate yourself, if you
have been hung up for years on your inability to forgive others,
ask yourself the question and be honest with the answer. The

man in the story was there for thirty-eight years. I am writing after thirty years. Where are you in the process? Would you like to get well? Would you like to move on to a different and better life? Would you like to have peace?

Notice the crippled man's answer to Jesus. "I can't sir." Read again why he can't, this time add a whiney voice. He has two excuses: "I have no one" and "someone else."

Notice he feels sorry for himself because "he has no one," and he blames everyone else around him. Self-pity and blame can and will control your life forever after a suicide death if you let it. Self-pity is absolutely destructive. Oswald Chambers calls it "satanic."[132] Why? Because it puts your focus, not on God, not on how to get well, not on moving forward, but on one thing—self. And self is never enough to overcome a suicide in your family.

The "someone else" excuse is blaming others. Blame doesn't work either. Your life will only move forward with Jesus Christ. Listen to his answer to the sick man: "Stand up, pick up your mat, and walk." Three verbs, three actions. The man had to do something in order to be healed: he had to believe the words of Jesus and be obedient. He had to think differently; no more "I can't" and "poor me." He attempted to stand up, and he attempted to pick up his mat. *Then* he walked.

You are crippled right now and have been for a long time, lying at the "Pool of Survival." Do you want to get well? Jesus has three answers for you also: Give up. Let go of your misery, the hatred, the loathing, the anger. Forgive. Remember, forgiveness does not take the relationship back to where it was at one time because the relationship has changed. It simply lets go of the haunting negatives that weigh you down. Forgiveness changes your mindset, moving from self-pity and blame to gratitude and joy. Unshackle yourself and forgive.

Now think about your own forgiveness. When Jesus taught his disciples how to pray, he taught them, " 'forgive us our sins, as we have forgiven those who sin against us.' "[133] Pretty clear directive from God, wouldn't you say?

Jesus forgives every single sin of yours, and he paid dearly for your absolution. In order for you to be free, Jesus left heaven, took on human flesh, was rejected by his own people, arrested, beaten, scourged, nailed to a cross, and died a horrible death, but he didn't stay in death's grip. God raised him from the dead, and he appeared alive to at least five hundred eyewitnesses.[134] Jesus ascended back into heaven and now prepares a heavenly home for your eternal joy. If he can do all that, he can help you forgive everyone you need to forgive, including yourself. It may take many attempts at forgiveness and months or even years to forgive completely, but with God all things are possible.[135]

Dear Jesus, I am crippled within my stubbornness to forgive. I desire in my heart to be healed, but my mind doesn't always think right. Forgive me, please, and because you forgive me, help me right now to forgive _____. Help me to let go of its negative hold on me. Help me through your power, Jesus, to be free from an unforgiving heart and mind. Help me give up my self-pity and blame. Change me to be more like you, Jesus—willing to forgive all sin for all time. Then your peace can flood in where the fury of unforgiveness has lived for so long in my heart and mind. I give it all up under your care, guidance, and protection. Keep satan and his lies away from me, oh, Lord. Give me your strength today. In the power of Jesus, I pray. Amen.

18

The Harvest Principle

Nathan was off to college, and Tom and I moved once again, this time closer to the mega church, and we became regular attenders. Up to that point, Tom and I had been "lurking in the balcony," but now we signed up for a membership class. Now they knew our names.

On the last day of class, I had a huge surprise. A sign-up card was given to everyone, requesting we choose our area of service within the church. If I had known that was going to happen, I would never have taken the class. (But you see how God is working here, don't you?)

I refused to fill in the blanks. Tom lovingly filled out his card and waited for me to do the same. I looked at him grimacing, brows furrowed, and whispered, "I'm not signing up for anything," and with a sweet face, I told the gentleman collecting the cards, "Oh, I'll fill this out later and bring it back."

"No, no, I'll wait for you," he smiled. "I'm not in any hurry. Just let us know where you plan to get involved. Go ahead. I'll wait."

Get involved? I'm not planning on getting involved!

My patient Tom whispered he had signed up to be a greeter at one of the church doors, and we would only have to stand there and say, "Good morning." He urged me to sign up for that too, and I did— while the lovely gentleman stood right in front of me, politely waiting.

Fast forward to our first Sunday as greeters: thank goodness we were stationed at a somewhat obscure door. But people entered. Tom smiled and said, "Good morning! We're so glad you are here," and extended his right hand.

It was my moment of decision. "Good morning" came out of my mouth, along with a smile even. But as soon as the attendees were past us, I looked at Tom, brows furrowed: "I am never doing this again!" Oops, another attender appeared, I cheerfully said, "Oh, good morning. Beautiful day, isn't it?" Big smile. As soon as they passed us, my head jerked, I looked at Tom, lips pursed, brows even more furrowed: "I am never doing this again!"

Honestly, our first greeter experience was hilarious. Rebellious, for sure. Maybe pathetic is a better description. But at least I was participating, at least as best I could at the time. I was still God's child. He had not disowned me, forgotten me, or abandoned me, and he allowed for my "baby step" of service to make inroads into my healing.

A Healing Truth — Sowing and harvesting will help transform your weeping into joy.

The book of Psalms came to my rescue again.

Those who sow with tears
  will reap with songs of joy.
Those who go out weeping,
  carrying seed to sow,
will return with songs of joy,
  carrying sheaves with them.[136]

The passage hit me like a ton of bricks. It held the answer for me: When you are too sad to be a part of anything good, you *can* cry and serve at the same time! But the person in the text also *did* something. He goes out crying *and* carrying seeds to sow. He *does* the work and returns, carrying sheaves. What do the sheaves represent? They are the results of his work. And what does the work produce? Songs of joy!

The weeping person is transformed into singing songs of joy through carrying the seeds, sowing them, and eventually harvesting the results—all while crying! The process of *doing the work* is what the weeping person needed, and the tragedy that provided the tears grows into a harvest of joy.

My dear friend, you and I are the ones weeping. And our tears need not keep us sidelined. Get involved in loving others. *Do* something. Take that first step in serving others: work in the nursery, paint a wall, help with babysitting, get involved with a food pantry ministry, help cook a meal at a homeless shelter, be a part of a small group, read to someone in hospice, set up chairs, wipe tables, serve coffee, give twenty bucks to a stranger, buy mittens for children, hand out bulletins, be a greeter, cut the neighbor's grass. Get involved in loving and serving others.

Every little action is sowing seeds. Every attempt at giving yourself away will produce a sheaf, which will give you joy. God will continue the healing process through your loving acts to others. You will harvest smiles, and a touch of joy will be your reward, I promise.

Anyone you know in this parable taught by Jesus?

> "A man with two sons told the older boy, 'Son, go out and work in the vineyard today.' The son answered, 'No, I won't go,' but later he changed his mind and went anyway. Then the father told the other son, 'You go,' and he said, 'Yes, sir, I will.' But he didn't go.
>
> "Which of the two obeyed his father?"
>
> They replied, "The first."[137]

Is that you? Have you said no to God when he calls you to get out of your misery? If you have, that's okay. He understands your pain and your heartache. But maybe it is time to change your mind. In my Bible, I have this little note: "Faith is the root. Love is the fruit." You didn't get this far reading this book without faith. Now it is your turn to make a decision. What will you do with your faith? Will you secure it within the vault of your headstrong heart, or will you share your faith freely, generously, and graciously?

Consider what the apostle Paul says: "Don't let evil conquer you, but conquer evil by doing good."[138] Sowing seeds of faith is good. Keeping your faith to yourself because of the hurt you've experienced is not good. That's letting evil get the best of you.

I get it. After a suicide death, you are filled with insecurity, and there are times you doubt your faith. On some days, you doubt everything. That is the battle! A simple first step, a prescription for moving forward, a path to joy is found in giving yourself away. *Do* something for someone else. *Be* thankful for what you still have in your life and share it with others. "Let us be concerned for one another, to help one another to show love and to do good."[139]

One of the best helpers Tom and I have is our "Thank You Book." It's just a simple paper notebook that we use each day to write down specific items we are thankful for. We number each entry. Each year we start a new book and begin a new list. Tom and I still have life, and we have blessings galore. Each day Tom and I notice God's generosity and thank him for it, even for the not-so-good things. Honestly, this is the latest entry— #1549 says: "Bumper sticker on guard rail, noticed at stop light: 'Avoid Religion. Follow Jesus.' (I told you, God has a sense of humor.)" I wonder what you would have on a list of things for which you are grateful? Whether the items are big or small doesn't matter. Gratitude can be a powerful antidote to bitterness, despair, and a host of other negative feelings and perspectives that can keep us from the much better life that God has for us.

What happened to the new greeters at the mega church? Tom and I eventually went on to become teachers in a fifth grade Sunday school class and leaders in a small group, a new members' class of all things.

Dear Jesus, I have often refused your call to serve, to help, to give myself away because I often think only of myself. Help me give love and care to others, exactly what I want people to give to me. Instead of wallowing in my heartache, help me get involved in a ministry. Help me overcome my selfishness and give myself away. With your help, I can sow the seeds of kindness, do the work before me, and reap the reward of joy. With your help, I can serve you by serving others. With your help, I will continue to heal and move forward in my new life filled with your grace. I love you, sweet Jesus, and in your name, I will serve. Amen.

19

Your New Name

S ometime in the late 1990s, God sent me a very precious gift. He made sure I heard a song written by D. J. Butler, "I Will Change Your Name." Written as though God is talking to you, God says he will change what you are known by: "wounded, outcast, lonely or afraid." He will give you a new name, such as "confidence, joyfulness, overcoming one."[140] I wondered if God would do that for me. How much I needed a new name that would give me hope that my life could be different, better, whole again.

After Matthew died, I felt overwhelmingly wounded by God—that he had given me more than I could bear with wounds so deep they would be impossible to heal. Along with deep pain, I found that grieving a suicide is a very lonely journey since no one comes to visit. No one calls. No one speaks about it. No one knows what to say, so they say nothing.

A very real blessing for Tom and me during our first year after Matthew's death was a neighborhood group of seven couples who all lived around the lake near our home. These couples gave us permission to laugh. On Friday nights, we would gather for a meal and play cards. A silly card game allowed me to laugh at a time when I thought I would never laugh again. Sometimes I could only handle an hour or two, and then Tom and I would just quietly slip out. The other couples understood and accepted us. I am forever grateful for their friendship.

What Tom and I discovered through this group is that we didn't need them to say anything. That surprised us. What we actually needed is just what they gave us: their company and especially their kindness through laughter.

Fear of losing our younger son Nathan gripped my heart during those first few years. I was so afraid of losing him that I hardly let him out of my sight, even though he was a teenage boy. He was learning to drive, active in sports and drama, dating, choosing a college—all normal activities. But fear hounded me. Every time he drove the car, I was filled with intense anxiety. Since I was relying only on self for those first years, my fear for Nathan's life was overbearing. It was inevitable that one more name would come to haunt me, and that was "Weary."

For me, it felt as though I was always wearing a full-length coat made out of lead. I had within me a sense of dissatisfaction and heaviness of heart. I could not balance my emotions or cast off the negativity. So I carried unresolved burdens around with me for years—"emotional baggage" as our culture calls it. Grieving great loss and suicide recovery are disorganized processes with little clarity. They are marked with a lot of confusion and often emotional numbness. Living in that tangled web produces weariness, a sense of heaviness, and an inability to resolve the issues that face us.

Have you ever seen an entertainer try to balance a plate on a wooden dowel? He gets the plate spinning on top of that dowel and works to keep it spinning. Then he adds another plate on another dowel and gets it spinning. He soon adds three plates, then four, and even more. All the while he has to strive to keep all the plates from falling. That is how I felt. I was trying to keep everything spinning in my life. And sometimes I managed it, for a while anyway. But the racing, the spinning, the trying to balance everything eventually came crashing down like china plates on concrete.

I found that trying to handle life this way was too much to bear. I needed help—divine help. I needed what Jesus offers to everyone: " 'Come to me, all of you who are weary and carry heavy burdens, and I will give you rest.' "[141] Oh, how I ached for rest and resolution. I don't remember how the words from Jesus took hold of my heart, but they did. " 'Take my yoke upon you,' " he added. " 'Let me teach you, because I am humble and gentle at heart, and you will find rest for your souls.' "[142] Oh, I so needed rest for my soul!

Read those comforting words again. What Jesus is saying to us is "Partner with me." That is the partnership that a yoke provides. One ox in a harness is often not enough to accomplish the job, but two linked together as a team can complete the more difficult, demanding tasks. Jesus is inviting us into this kind of relationship with him. He wants to partner with us to get through those burdens that weigh us down so much.

Notice also that Jesus says, "Let me teach you." Daily, he will teach you truth in the Word of God. But this starts with a first step: Be teachable. You must be willing to hear and receive, to learn and apply. Read his words to us in the New Testament Gospels (Matthew, Mark, Luke, and John). If you attend a Bible-believing church, you can find enrichment there from God's Word also.

Part of what I have learned from Jesus has come from reading the name he has for those who trust him and believe in him. In Luke, Jesus says, " 'Let the children come to me. ... For the Kingdom of God belongs to those who are like these children.' "[143] The apostle John states, "See how very much our Father loves us, for he calls us his children, and that is what we are!"[144]

A Healing Truth — God has a new name chosen for you. Come and claim it!

This is great news for all suicide survivors. And not only does he have a new name for you, but you get to choose the name that sounds right for you!

The last book of the Bible has a beautiful picture for us to see. In Revelation 3, Jesus says: " 'Look, I stand at the door and knock. If you hear my voice and open the door, I will come in, and we will share a meal together as friends. Those who are victorious will sit with me on my throne, just as I was victorious and sat with my Father on his throne.' "[145]

Different Bible translations use different names for the one whom Jesus is describing here as "victorious." Some versions say victor or victorious one, others say conqueror, while some say overcomer. Which name do you prefer? You may not feel ready to accept your new name, but I want you to think ahead. Will your name be *The Victor*? Or maybe you prefer *The One Who Conquers*.

The name I chose is *Overcoming One*, which comes directly from the song by D. L. Baker. Every time I sang that song, which I did often, I began thinking of myself as *Overcoming One*. I was determined to overcome my intense suffering, confusion, and sadness. In my mind, I pictured Jesus healing me and giving me his new name for me. Then I pictured him drawing that name on the palms of his hands, just as Isaiah describes it: " 'See, I have written your name on the palms of my hands—[Overcoming One]."[146] That vision of what Jesus was doing for me helped shape my future. It gave me a new definition of myself. It helped me come alongside Jesus in a new way and depend on him to help me lift and carry my burdens. Not only did he claim me as his own child, a daughter of the King, he acknowledged my pain and my struggles. And just as he endured suffering, he understood my suffering. Just as he overcame death, he gave me life!

The most meaningful and beautiful picture God has ever given to me comes from Revelation 3:21. I especially treasure how it comes across in the Amplified Bible version: "He who overcomes [the world through believing that Jesus is the Son of God], I will grant to him [the privilege] to sit beside Me on My throne, as I also overcame and sat down beside My Father on His throne." Just imagine that moment in heaven when you, as a believer in Jesus Christ and an Overcomer, a Victor, a Conqueror, get called by Christ to share his throne. You, my forgiven and healed friend, will walk forward to claim your promised reward. Jesus will lovingly make room for you on his throne. He will motion for you to take the seat right next to him.

Our Father will nod with approval.

The angels will sing with delight.

Jesus will smile.

You will then fully and completely realize the great love God has for you and the perfect gift of his grace. To those who overcome through faith and hope in Christ, you will finally have eternal healing and eternal rest.

———

Dearest Jesus, I am humbled by your love and grace for me, and I do receive you into my heart, my mind, and my life. I desire complete healing from the battles fought during this time of suicide survival. I surrender my life to you. Give me all that I need to become an Overcomer, a Victor, a Conqueror. I am yours, in the name of my beautiful Savior. Help me to partner daily with you and allow your Spirit free reign in my life. What joy will be mine! Amen.

20

Resist, Resolve, Rejoice

I t's good for you to grieve, but not forever.

It's good for you to journey through the struggle, but not forever.

You need to keep moving forward, even if the steps are small.

There is a great life waiting for you—a life living in the fullness of God. He desires to bless you with healing, peace, rest, and ultimately, joy. I know this is true. Take this Bible passage to heart:

> "For I know the plans I have for you"—this is the LORD's declaration—"plans for your welfare, not for disaster, to give you a future and a hope. You will call to Me and come and pray to Me, and I will listen to you. You will seek Me and find Me when you search for Me with all your heart."[147]

Over and over in the Bible, God promises forgiveness, power, rest, joy, and the provision of his protection and guidance. His promises abound in the Bible. They are just waiting for you to find them and embrace them. They will be the path for you on this journey. They will be God's guidance for you, day in and day out. They are your guarantee of recovery.

Three Essential Words

As you come toward the end of this book, I have three words to help you: resist, resolve, rejoice. They capsulize three essential steps toward your path to healing, peace, and rest.

First of all, *resist* satan. I have described my journey as a battle, and it is. I can find no other way to accurately describe it. In this battle, satan will keep striking out to trick you, tempt you, tire you, and test you. He can be relentless. In this fight, remember this timeless word of advice from Jesus's half-brother, James: "Humble yourselves before God. Resist the devil, and he will flee from you."[148]

With Jesus, you have the power of God working in you. And satan battles to hinder that divine power. But you can stop him. You must put satan in his place, and that place is under the authority of Jesus Christ. Jesus is always greater and more powerful than satan. Jesus always has dominion over satan. So here's how you actually resist satan with Jesus at the helm. When you are upset, confused, scared, weary, angry, sad, or tempted in any way, and you need God's power, simply say the name of Jesus. Whisper, or better yet, say out loud, "Jesus, Jesus, Jesus." Or, do what I do: I tell satan, "In the name of Jesus, leave me alone, or bow and worship Jesus with me." He will flee. He must flee because he knows Jesus has all authority in heaven and earth.[149] Stating the authority of Jesus works to resist the devil's lies, and it will make a huge difference in how you think and feel.

This came across my computer screen the other day: "The next time satan reminds you of your past, remind him of his future."[150] And that future for him is God's promised judgment of him as expressed in Revelation 20:10—namely, that he will have a fiery, punishing end forever and ever. "The God of peace"—the God we trust and worship—"will soon crush Satan under [our] feet."[151] That is God's special promise for all believers, including those of us who are suicide survivors.

Resolve is the second word I want you to recall. Take a stand today. Make an honest decision and determination. Say out loud, "I will heal, and I will have joy in my life." Surviving a suicide is ugly and painful and difficult, and if you stay in that negative mindset, you will be defeated in your battle to survive. Instead, resolve to have a fixed purpose, be intentional, remain steadfast on your road to recovery. Tell yourself over and over, "I am determined to heal, and God will help me, no matter how long it takes." As part of your resolve, choose Bible verses that speak to you and memorize them. Repeat them often. Use them as your prayers. Think about those words throughout the day. Tape them on the dashboard of your car. Put them where you will see them often.

If you have just recently lost a loved one to suicide, please be patient and kind to yourself. You must grieve and weep and allow the Holy Spirit to comfort you and strengthen you. This is the time for you to rest, pray, and mourn. Acting with resolve in this stage of your journey can involve choosing to read something out of your Bible every day. I would encourage you to start with the book of Psalms. You might also find value in some devotionals. Through it all, remember that Jesus prays for you. "He is forever able to save the people he leads to God, because he always lives to speak to God for them."[152] Rest in the Lord and stay close to him, and your healing will increase.

The third essential word to recall is *rejoice*. Rejoice in your tiny triumphs, those first steps you have already accomplished. Rejoice that you stuck with me and read this entire book. Find something right now for which you can praise and thank God. Find something that brings you happiness, and thank God for it. Yes, there is something to be grateful for. Search, seek, look, and find it. Your spirit of thanksgiving will do so much to help return joy to your life. Today you could even start your own "Thank You Book."

Proverbs 15:30 tells us, "A cheerful look brings joy to the heart." Find something to look at that will bring joy to your heart. Years ago, I would go into the Hallmark shop and read the funny Shoebox greeting cards when they were first introduced, and they would make me laugh. Some days Tom and I just laugh—for no reason at all. Try it, for several seconds, just giggle and guffaw out loud. You will feel better.

The Good and Renewed Life

There is life after suicide. While the wound of suicide never goes away, you can enter a new chapter in your life. "God can do anything, you know—far more than you could ever imagine or guess or request in your wildest dreams!"[153] Tom and I experienced God do just that for us.

In 1999, God moved Tom and me to a foreign country; well, it was not really on foreign soil, but it seemed like that to us. You see, we moved to the Deep South, where we were acquainted with only two people—Tom's new boss and his wife. In the spirit of the South, we were fixin' to start a new life. It was a complete change for us, a new chapter in our book of life. While there, God continued his healing process within us.

Five days after we arrived in our new location, we worshiped at a large church and listened to a sermon on "God's Wheel." That was what the wording sounded like to us at first. The sermon was about God's will, but "will" came across to us as "wheel." We were learning that southern touch to English.

Two days after our first visit, the pastor's wife called our home and invited me to lunch. I couldn't believe it. How did she get my phone number ... and so quickly? On the phone, she casually mentioned that she was finally back at work after her son's death in a car accident. I was stunned! In one week's time, on foreign soil, God had sent someone to me who would understand a child's death.

"Oh, we lost a son also," I blurted out, quite to my surprise. That was something I *never* said in a first conversation, for this very reason: the inevitable follow-up question was "How did your son die?" That was my moment of panic. I couldn't believe that I had actually told this woman about Matthew. You see, I had secretly longed for our move to be a fresh start for us, a new beginning, a new era where we would not be overshadowed by suicide. *I won't tell anyone about it*, I told myself before we left the North. *No one really has to know.*

Now I was stuck. And I couldn't lie. "He took his own life," I responded, tears forming in my eyes. *Elaine*, I thought, *why didn't you just keep your mouth shut?* I berated myself, and all of this within a matter of a few seconds.

"Ohhh, that happened to some dear friends of ours, Ron and Kaye Dunn," she replied with concern and interest in her voice. "He's a pastor too, and he's written a book about their experience." It was *the* Ron Dunn who had met Tom and me at the mega church, now seven hundred miles away and three years in the past. He was the one who had told us, "You will have joy again in your life."

The God of all creation, King of kings and Lord of lords, the Beginning and the End had gone to great lengths to bring about this very moment in time: two strangers meeting on a phone, talking for the first time, giving assurance of joy to my life. The God of the universe had given me this moment—a time of blessing that I could have never imagined! I knew, and without the slightest doubt, that God had me on the path he had created for me.

After her phone call, I laid on the floor and wept. I reveled in God's joy and plan for my life, and I understood his deep love for me. I finally grasped what Job meant when he said to God, " 'I know that You can do all things, and that no plan is impossible for You.' "[154]

One of my favorite verses may be one you didn't expect: "And we know that God causes everything to work together for the good of those who love God and are called according to his purpose for them."[155] I've struggled with that verse for years. In my rebellion, I kept thinking, *Nothing good will ever come out of Matthew's death.* But I was so arrogant and so wrong. I have repented of those thoughts many times over. Here is what I came to see: *God isn't obligated to tell us what the good is concerning our loved one's suicide, but there is good.* Why do I know that God's goodness will prevail? For at least three good reasons, just as Romans 8:28 says:

- We love God.
- We are called to be his forgiven children.
- We were created for a purpose.

God will bring good even out of your loved one's suicide. I have seen him do that through Matthew's death. He will do that for you too.

God is with us and for us. Even after the loss of a loved one. He does not abandon us, and his plan for us includes his love, his goodness, his mercy and grace, his compassion and healing, and his commitment to see us through anything this world throws at us.

Go to him.

Lean on him.

Partner with him.

Open up your heart and hurt to him.

He is with you, and he is for you.

My prayer for you is what Paul prayed for so many centuries ago. Right now you may think what he asks for could never be a part of your life, at least not now. But I know in the core of my being that what he asks for can be real in your life. It can help you find and experience the next chapter of your life—if you want it. So with the apostle Paul, I say to you: "I pray that God, the source of hope, will fill you completely with joy and peace because you trust in him. Then you will overflow with confident hope through the power of the Holy Spirit."[156]

One day, I will meet you in heaven where there will be a grand reunion—you, me, and all our loved ones, invited and called and forgiven by Jesus Christ. If I don't see you on this side of heaven, I will join you later. Until then, resist, resolve, and rejoice.

Grace Always Wins!

Believing Grace, receiving Grace.
Fresh, daily Grace.
Forgiveness wrapped around me ... now!
A Garment of Salvation,
A Robe of Righteousness.
Fresh, generous, glorious Grace.
God's eternal gift ... ALL MINE!
GRACE. Always more than I will ever need.
God's favor, God's love
By God decreed, and through Christ
Guaranteed.

A Personal Note from Elaine

Dear friends,

There is a definite connection between us. I know there is. You see, I have been praying for you for years. When I sat down for the first time to write about my journey, I prayed for you, and that began on August 1, 2018.

It was difficult for me to write at first because it took me back into my deep pain. I had to relive the sad and difficult times of hurt and anguish. I cried a lot during those writing times, but along with the tears, I prayed for you. I know, without a moment of hesitation, that God loves me and gave me the words to put on paper. I also know that God loves you and cares for you deeply. His heart's desire is for you to be healed!

As my book progressed, I struggled with decisions about which battles I would share with you. God led me to write about forgiveness and grace, but I first had to better understand my obsessive guilt, blame, and rejection. That was painful to work through. It was my dark side, and I was sometimes afraid to share it. But then I thought of you and your pain and struggles. I prayed for you, always asking God to lead me in my writing so that you, my precious friends, could know I understand and love you and that it is also my heart's desire for you to be healed.

Won't you please continue the journey with me? I have a simple website for you to keep in touch with me. It's just my name, elainekennelly.com. Please subscribe, and I will send you a personal letter every month, sharing new things I have learned and inspirational truths that will continue your healing journey. I will have a blog on the website too. Of course, you will always find prayers for you, along with poems and other thoughts to help you and those you know along the way. I would treasure your prayers for me also. We are in this journey together.

Blessings to all in Jesus Christ,

Elaine

P.S. God has already given me another writing assignment—a devotional book that will help all those who have lost a loved one to suicide. Watch the website for details. It will be coming—covered in prayer again!

Acknowledgments

Many people have influenced and encouraged me along my journey of surviving a suicide loss. The most important and most helpful has been my sweet-spirited husband, Tom. Together, we lived through the storm. Together, we walked where no one we knew had walked, with no clear understanding of how to walk. On some days, our walk turned into a crawl. But we still took the journey together. Thank you, Tom, for your patient love and kindness during an overwhelming and difficult journey. God used you more than anyone to help me heal. You truly are my sweetheart, my soul mate, my best friend. I love you with all my heart!

To Nathan, the sunshine of our lives, I thank you for being the positive, happy child you were even when Matthew got all the negative attention. You have lived with the mindset of finding good everywhere. Thank you! Your consistent reminders that I was a great mom have brightened my days, and I am forever grateful for a son like you. Thank you for bringing

Kayla, Kennon, and Kaven into our lives and family. We are rejoicing grandparents!

My sincere thanks goes to Bill Watkins of Literary Solutions who kindly took me under his wing. He graciously consented to edit every sentence to make it better. He made me dig deep into my thoughts and emotions to bring out the best in my writing. Bill, I am grateful, not only for your editing expertise, but for your gentleness along the way. I count you as a friend.

Thank you to my sweet friend Sarah DeLazzer. You never gave up on me and consistently made me feel that my words on paper touch hearts for Jesus. Thank you, dear sister in the Lord, for giving me the labels of "writer" and "author" when my own mind was not that generous. Your "Something Sister" Bible study still continues to lead women to know Jesus better and love him more. Praise God!

Tim and Lisa O'Hara—you are precious people, and my heartfelt appreciation for your loving friendship is alive and well. Your insight, perspective, and diligence in seeing a need for this story to be told paved the way for success. I love you both.

Thank you to my long-time friend, Andrea Thoenes, for years of mentoring me to be the child of God he desires in my faith walk with him. You, as a gifted writer yourself, have encouraged me to persist in sharing God's love and grace to so many hurting people.

To Morgan James Publishing, I give a heartfelt thanks for being the key instrument in God's lovely plan. You have graciously partnered with me to send healing truths all over the world to help those hurting after a suicide loss. Terry Whalin and Stephanie MacLawhorn have been especially helpful, kind, and concerned. They, too, understand the need for this book, and I am grateful.

There are countless people to appreciate, but the real credit goes to my heavenly Father for his love and determination to get this book written to help others and give them hope. His heart's desire became mine. His grace covered Matthew. His grace covers me. All praise and thanks to him!

LORD … all we have accomplished is really from you.
Isaiah 26:12

About the Author

Elaine Kennelly is a mom who lost an eighteen-year-old son to suicide. But she cannot be defined by that alone. She is also an accomplished businesswoman who for eighteen years ran an award-winning Hallmark Gold Crown store in Hartford, Wisconsin. During that time, she created her own cable TV show, *Elaine's World,* which was very successful locally. Her entrepreneurial spirit moved to the South with her, and she successfully put together a team to start a Keller Williams Realty Market Center in Huntsville, Alabama, which has expanded and still flourishes. Elaine is not afraid to plant herself wherever she lives—doing, creating, writing, and teaching.

Elaine graduated from Concordia University in Chicago, with a degree in elementary education and a minor in theology. She loves to learn from Scripture and teach it to others. Books she has written include *Something Sisters 31 Day Devotional* and *Faith Over Feelings*. She also created a website, *somethingsisters.com*. She loves to write poetry that shares God's character, especially his grace and love. Tom and she are active participants in many ministries, but one of their favorites has been facilitating GriefShare classes.

Her friends describe her as a vibrant and vivacious person who loves to laugh. You would never really see her scars when you meet her, but they are there.

Elaine now resides in Loveland, Colorado, with the love of her life, Tom. They enjoy living there, discovering all the beauty Colorado has to offer, including their lovely family, complete with two grandsons.

Endnotes

1   Psalm 88:18.

2   Genesis 4:1–12.

3   Genesis 1:26–28; Psalm 8:5.

4   Genesis 2.

5   Genesis 3:1–19; Revelation 12:7–9.

6   Genesis 3:15.

7   Genesis 4:1–2.

8   Genesis 4:3–5.

9   Genesis 4:6–7 CEV.

10   1 Peter 5:8.

11   Genesis 1:31.

12   Genesis 4:10 GNT.

13   Ephesians 1:4.

14   Titus 1:2.

15   Mark 9:24 GNT.

16   Psalm 94:17 NIV.

17   Proverbs 18:14 GNT.

18 Psalm 94:18–19 NIV.

19 Deuteronomy 29:29.

20 Wayne Grudem, Systematic Theology (Grand Rapids, MI: Zondervan, 1994), 217.

21 Psalm 115:3 HCSB.

22 Job 42:2 CEV.

23 Jeremiah 32:27 CEV.

24 Exodus 3:14.

25 Romans 11:33–36 MSG.

26 Isaiah 55:8–9.

27 Romans 8:38–39 TLB.

28 Acts 16:31.

29 John 1:12.

30 Hebrews 10:22.

31 James 4:8.

32 Zephaniah 3:17 NIV.

33 Luke 1:37 GW.

34 Oswald Chambers, My Utmost for His Highest, updated edition, ed. James Reimann (Grand Rapids, MI: Discovery House, 1992), September 18.

35 Luke 4:3.

36 Luke 4:5–13.

37 Titus 1:2; Hebrews 6:18.

38 Joshua 1:5 NIV.

39 Psalm 46:1.

40 Psalm 139:1–18; Jeremiah 23:23–24; Hebrews 4:13.

41 John 14:6.

42 Deuteronomy 30:19–20.

43 Chambers, My Utmost for His Highest, December 31.

44 Psalm 51:10–12 GW.

45 Psalm 88:3–4, 7–9, 13–14, 18 NIV.

46 Sarah Young, Jesus Calling (Nashville: Thomas Nelson, 2008), December 25.

47 Isaiah 53:2–4.

48 Mark 14:34 GNT.

49 Matthew 27:46 NIV.

50 Psalm 77:1–2 NIV.

51 Psalm 13:1–2.

52 Psalm 42:9 NIV.

53 Psalm 6:1–3.

54 Psalm 147:3.

55 Psalm 116:15.

56 Psalm 119:81.

57 Psalm 145:14.

58 Psalm 16:7–8.

59 Psalm 145:18.

60 William P. Young, The Shack (Newberry Park, CA: Windblown Media, 2007), 21.

61 Author's personal adaptation to the parable of the Prodigal Son found in Luke 15:11–24.

62 Psalm 73:2, 21, 23–26.

63 Genesis 3:14 CEV.

64 Genesis 3:15 CEV.

65 John 3:16–18 CEV.

66 John 5:24.

67 John 3:18 CEV.

68 Romans 3:22 TLB.

69 Job 1:1–3.

70   Job 1:12.

71   Job 2:6–7.

72   Job 2:9.

73   Romans 3:10–12.

74   Job 38:2–3.

75   Psalm 25:14 NKJV.

76   Chambers, My Utmost for His Highest, June 3.

77   Ruth and Warren Myers, 31 Days of Praise (Colorado Springs: Multnomah Books, 1994), 76.

78   Emphasis added.

79   Genesis 16:2 NIV.

80   Genesis 16:10.

81   Chambers, My Utmost for His Highest, January 12.

82   James 1:2–3.

83   Philippians 4:13.

84   Psalm 139:13–16 TLB.

85   Genesis 1:31 TLB.

86   Ephesians 2:10.

87   Genesis 3:15; Matthew 25:34; John 17:24; Ephesians 1:4; Titus 1:2; 1 Peter 1:18–20.

88   Matthew 9:11–13.

89   Matthew 23.

90   John 12:4–6.

91   Matthew 26:14–16.

92   Matthew 26:49.

93   Matthew 26:50.

94   Matthew 27:3–4.

95   Ephesians 2:8.

96   Romans 10:11 NLT, HCSB, and ESV.

97   Romans 10:13.

98   Romans 5:21.

99   Timothy Keller, The Prodigal Prophet: Jonah and the Mystery of God's Mercy (New York: Viking, 2018), 211.

100 Romans 8:1.

101 John 6:47 CEV.

102 Proverbs 17:15.

103 1 Corinthians 4:3–5, emphasis added.

104 Acts 7:54–8:1.

105 1 Corinthians 4:4–5.

106 Romans 14:8–10, 12–13.

107 2 Peter 3:8.

108 Isaiah 61:10.

109 Jonah 1:2–3 MSG.

110 Jonah 2:1 MSG.

111 John 9:2–3 NIV.

112 1Corinthians 13:7 GW.

113 Deuteronomy 30:15, 19–20.

114 Psalm 45:7 NIV.

115 Henry T. Blackaby and Claude V. King, Experiencing God (Nashville: Broadman & Holman, 1994), 41.

116 Psalm 18:35 AMP.

117 1 John 3:1 NIV.

118 Rick Warren, "What You Think, You Are," Daily Hope Devotional, January 24, 2019, https://pastorrick.com/what-you-think-you-are/.

119 Chambers, My Utmost for His Highest, October 10.

120 Daniel 1:8.

121 Daniel 1:8, 12–13.

122 Daniel 1:15.

123 Romans 12:2.

124 Deuteronomy 29:15.

125 Matthew 22:36–38; Deuteronomy 6:4–5; Leviticus 19:18; 1 John 4:7–21.

126 A paraphrase of 1 Chronicles 28:20.

127 2 Chronicles 16:9.

128 Matthew 13:16.

129 Isaiah 5:18.

130 Philippians 4:12–13.

131 John 5:5–8, emphasis added.

132 Chambers, My Utmost for His Highest, August 20.

133 Matthew 6:12.

134 1 Corinthians 15:6.

135 Matthew 19:26.

136 Psalm 126:5–6 NIV.

137 Matthew 21:28–31.

138 Romans 12:21.

139 Hebrews 10:24 GNT.

140 D. J. Butler, lyricist and vocalist, "I Will Change Your Name," Mercy/Vineyard Publishing, 1987.

141 Matthew 11:28.

142 Matthew 11:29.

143 Luke 18:16.

144 1 John 3:1.

145 Revelation 3:20–21.

146 Isaiah 49:16, the words "Overcoming One" are added by the author.

147 Jeremiah 29:11–13 HCSB.

148 James 4:7.

149 Matthew 28:18; 11:27.

150 Bible Study Tools.com, February 4, 2015.

151 Romans 16:20.

152 Hebrews 7:25 CEV.

153 Ephesians 3:20 MSG.

154 Job 42:2 NASB.

155 Romans 8:28.

156 Romans 15:13.